The Political Economy of Gunnar Myrdal

T0271683

The intellectual trajectory of Gunnar Myrdal, Swedish Nobel Laureate economist, sociologist, and politician, brings us through many of the major issues in the world economy and politics of the twentieth century. This new volume explores Myrdal's work on three major themes:

- breaking away from conventional assumptions in Political Economy (and highlighting flaws that can still be found in today's teachings on political economy);
- finding ways of re-creating Europe after the Second World War, including the discussions between liberal Americans and European social democrats on how to create a more cooperative and socially just international order;
- and understanding the impact of environmental concerns on growth and development, starting with Myrdal's participation in the first UN Conference on Environment in Stockholm 1960 and continuing with his later writings.

What then is the relevance of these themes today? Today, in these times when financial crisis threatens to block international and domestic economies, when the European Union's promises of prosperity and cooperation seem to be severely threatened and when there is a large consensus that current modes of economic development are ecologically unsustainable. Can we find ways of transcending seemingly intractable dilemmas? These questions will be discussed in the final part of the book.

Örjan Appelqvist is Associate Professor in the Department of Economic History at the University of Stockholm, Sweden.

Routledge frontiers of political economy

The Political Economy of Gunnar Myrdal

Transcending dilemmas post-2008

Örjan Appelqvist

Routledge
Taylor & Francis Group

LONDON AND NEW YORK

First published 2014
by Routledge
2 Park Square, Milton Park, Abingdon, Oxfordshire OX14 4RN

and by Routledge
711 Third Avenue, New York, NY 10017

First issued in paperback 2016

Routledge is an imprint of the Taylor & Francis Group, an informa business

© 2014 Örjan Appelqvist

British Library Cataloguing in Publication Data
A catalogue record for this book is available from the British Library

Library of Congress Cataloging in Publication Data
Appelqvist, Örjan.
The Political Economy of Gunnar Myrdal: Transcending Dilemmas Post-2008/Örjan Appelqvist.
    pages cm
    1. Myrdal, Gunnar, 1898–1987. 2. Economists–Sweden. 3. Economics.
    I. Title.
    HB179.S8M9736 2013
    330.092–dc23

                                                              2013020574

ISBN 13: 978-1-138-24380-4 (pbk)
ISBN 13: 978-0-415-52714-9 (hbk)

Typeset in Times
by Wearset Ltd, Boldon, Tyne and Wear

Contents

Introduction

Francis O. Wilcox, Dean of the John Hopkins University in Washington, was asked in 1969 why he had called on Gunnar Myrdal to conduct a study on *Challenge of World* Poverty, Wilcox referred to Gunnar Myrdal's several careers as university professor, minister of government and head of the UN Economic Commission for Europe. He said: 'With this background he is admirably equipped to bridge the gap between the academician and the policy maker, to temper theory with practice and to offer meaningful suggestions about tomorrow's world.'[1] Some 40 years later those reasons for Gunnar Myrdal's relevance are still valid.

It is true that by his intellectual and political trajectory Gunnar Myrdal worked on many of the century's most vital questions. In connection with the publication of *The Essential Gunnar Myrdal* in 2005 the eminent US economist John Kenneth Galbraith wrote: 'Gunnar Myrdal taught me more about economics and its human and social impact than anyone else in his generation. Indeed of any recent generation. He is more relevant now than ever. In fact, he defines the time and the century, including what has gone wrong.'[2]

This relevance and depth of Gunnar Myrdal's economic and social analyses has been the subject of several valuable publications.[3] He has left us a rich intellectual heritage. But its richness is such that it has to be re-evaluated from time to time. And the results will not be identical: the river that we enter is never quite the same. Indeed – one of the guiding motives of the present re-assessment of the approach of Gunnar Myrdal to political economy is that we are now living in a political, economic and social landscape fundamentally different from that of the preceding 40 years. A landscape structured by the crisis in the global financial-economic system as well as the growing pressures of the ecological crisis. Two recent events illustrate this fundamental change of the political and economic landscape: the bankruptcy of the Lehman Brothers in August 2008 and the failure of the UN Conference on Environment in Copenhagen in 2009 to reach any binding commitment regarding climate change.

The Lehman crash because it unleashed a chain of reactions which put the whole system of the world economy at the brink of collapse, and because it triggered a crisis process the effects of which we are still living with today, and we are still only at the beginning of this crisis. The failure (or the disguised collapse) of the UN Conference in Copenhagen likewise illustrated this fundamental change of political climate because it demonstrated in a drastic way the hidden conflict embedded within environmental issues: the distribution of power. The delegations from Europe, United States, China and South America had deeply conflicting views of who should pay the ecological debts. Consequently, the ecological crisis has deep geo-political and social implications, implications that could be compared with the deep conflict regarding the world poverty issue raised by Gunnar Myrdal some 50 years ago.

One of the starting points of this re-assessment is the conviction that these two are watershed events that will – or should – structure our approach to social, economic and political issues in the years to come. It is with this conviction in mind that the relevance of Myrdal's ideas will be assessed.

Gunnar Myrdal's ideas will also be discussed with special emphasis on political issues. One of the most remarkable features of his work is the alternation between the roles of researcher, politician and opinion maker. Although analysing his contributions to science history and the history of ideas is a fascinating topic in itself it only partially captures the extent of his endeavour. It is only by understanding the political passion that was animating him (and his wife and collaborator Alva Myrdal) that the focus of his interest and intellectual development can be properly understood. This very rare alternation of professional roles touches on a still deeper level of problems: that of the relationship between science and society. Under what circumstances can scientific knowledge translate into social change?

If there is a lacuna in the general understanding of Gunnar Myrdal's work it lies in this political dimension. Partly this is due to the fact that his most passionately political work, *Varning för fredsoptimism* (Warning for Post-War Optimism) was never published in English and was subsequently overshadowed by his active participation in the Swedish post-war Social-Democratic government.

Reading this book as a PhD student changed my scientific orientation. What I found was a novel analysis of the internal changes in the US economy brought about by the war effort, a passionate introduction to the liberal US debates on how to organize world trade after the war and on how to avoid yet another disastrous Versailles Treaty settlement. It was drastically different from the received, conventional wisdom of the history of the later years of the Second World War and the subsequent Cold War period. Written before the possibility of hindsight it offered a vivid understanding of the openness and uncertainty of that period. It gave me a long-standing scepticism against established historiographies based on memoirs and rear-view mirror writings. Their determinism is illusory; history as it happens is always open, shaped by human hopes and fears. And history is always conditioned by the perceptions of the individual and its significance is moulded by the circumstances of the present: it needs to be re-searched. As Gunnar Myrdal constantly teaches us, we are all biased.

Gunnar Myrdal's outlook and fundamental research questions were formulated against the backdrop of the 1929 Wall Street crisis and its sequels in the ensuing Depression era. The general question I would like to address in this book can be framed thus: in what ways can Myrdal's critique of dominating, conventional economic theory, and his approach to science in general and economic and social problems of that time in particular, be of value in confronting challenges posed by the present crisis process?

It would be far too ambitious to try to cover the whole range of problems triggered by the financial crisis of 2008. The text will therefore concentrate on the European dimension of the problems, mainly dealing with its macro-economic aspects. First because the social and economic woes of the European Union are the locus of the world economy where the contradictions caused by the crisis stands out most acutely, exposing conflicts between the financial needs of servicing public debts of the countries of the European Union and the social needs of their populations. Such contradictions are threatening the basic fabric of their welfare societies, a true 'European Dilemma'. Second this focus would appear appropriate since Gunnar Myrdal was one of the most prominent architects of the post-war welfare societies and was deeply implicated in the regional post-war reconstruction of Europe.

The first chapter of the book will focus on Gunnar Myrdal's early years as economist in Sweden. The development of his critique of basic assumptions of neo-classical economic theory, his explanation of the role of values in science and the steps taken towards a dynamic understanding of economic and social processes.

The second chapter examines the development of his ideas on international economy, taking his 'post-war manifesto' as a starting point. This section will follow his endeavours as head of the UN Economic Commission for Europe, his broadening approach to global development problems and trade issues, his major study of the many impediments to modernization and social development in South Asia and finally his last broad international work, *Challenge of World Poverty*. With reference to the ecological crisis we will also highlight his far-sightedness in this field. As early as 1969, in his speech in connection with the first UN Conference on Human Environment he pointed very clearly to the ecological dangers and dilemmas involved.

These two chapters will provide us with the tools needed for the discussion of the crisis of 2008 and patterns and dilemmas of the present crisis process. This discussion will single out and reaffirm the basic tenets of Gunnar Myrdal's theoretical propositions that seem indispensible to those in search of socially acceptable solutions of the actual social and economic crisis of the European Union. It will also indicate the areas where his ideas – and even more the conventional ones – need to be transcended if the European dilemma is to be solved.

Notes

1 G. Myrdal, *The Challenge of World Poverty: A World Anti-Poverty Program in Outline* (London: Allen Lane, 1970), Foreword, p. ix.
2 Ö. Appelqvist, S. Andersson (eds), *The Essential Gunnar Myrdal* (New York:New Press, 2005).
3 Among the general overviews published in English most notably G. Dostaler, D. Ethier, L. Lepage (eds), *Gunnar Myrdal and his works* (Montreal: Harvest House Publishers, 1992) and W.J. Barber, *Gunnar Myrdal: An Intellectual Biography* (London: Palgrave, 2008). Specifically Myrdal's early contributions as a social scientist in Sweden and the US are covered in Walter A. Jackson, *Gunnar Myrdal and America's Conscience: Social Engerneering and Racial Liberalism, 1938–1987* (Chapel Hill and London: University of North Carolina Press, 1990). At the height of neo-liberal hubris in the 1990s James Angresano argued the value of Myrdal's institutional approach in *The Political Economy of Gunnar Myrdal: An Institutional Basis for the Transformation Problem* (Cheltenham: Edward Elgar, 1997).

1 Explaining fundamentals in the intellectual development of Gunnar Myrdal

What were the basic lines of development of Gunnar Myrdal's ideas on economics and society? This question will now be examined in this chapter which will trace the interplay between published works and professional occupations during the first 20 years of Myrdal's career.

Gunnar Myrdal was born in Solvarbo in the Swedish province of Dalarna in 1898. Dalarna is a rural province dominated by peasant freeholders and local tradesmen. He was the son of a self-made entrepreneur in the construction business and the first of his family to receive higher education. Myrdal often prided himself on his roots in Dalarna, a province with a reputation for the stubbornness and nationalism of its population.[1]

More important still was the lifelong emotional and intellectual partnership he experienced with his wife Alva Myrdal (born Reimers). He met her as a young student in 1919 and they formed an intellectual couple that soon became the centre of a 'modernist' and reform-minded circle of intellectuals and artists in Stockholm. Throughout his life this relationship and Alva's contributions were of vital importance to his development: not only in creating the Myrdalian worldview generally, but also at several specific occasions in reorienting his energies. In certain areas – those of family policies and educational matters, and later regarding disarmament issues – her expertise was guiding him. Since the focus of this book is the development of Myrdal's ideas on economic theory the importance of this relationship is only signalled here.[2]

Gunnar Myrdal started his university studies as a law student, graduating in 1923. Then – and notably on Alva Myrdal's advice – he decided to study political economy, a subject that she believed had greater impact in solving the problems of the time.[3]

The issue of valuations in science and economics

When the Gunnar Myrdal started his career as a young economist in the mid-1920s in Sweden, Stockholm was a centre for several economists of great renown in the neo-classical tradition. The economic historian Eli Heckscher had formulated his theory on the role of free trade in international relations, theories later being expanded into the Heckscher–Ohlin theorem.[4] David Davidson's quantitative theory on monetary policy was widely recognized as the conventional view to combat inflation in the wake of the post-war turmoil. Gunnar Myrdal's tutor, Gustav Cassel, Professor of Political Economy and Financial Sciences[5] at the University of Stockholm, was an unquestioned authority on political economy.

Cassel's major work, 'Theory on Social Economy'[6] intended to make the study of economics truly scientific by discarding the theory of values altogether and by making the theory of prices the sole rock upon which a proper understanding of the production of material necessities was founded.Such a theory, devoid of the philosophical issues that were at the heart of forerunners such as Adam Smith and John Stuart Mill, was of course more suited to the full-fledged mathematician Gustav Cassel.Without such a theory, Cassel declared that the only things that Social Reformers could produce were 'cheap speculations on the social organization of the future or costly disturbances of the very delicate machinery of present economic life'.[7]

Given these circumstances, and given the ardent commitment of the Myrdal couple to 'social reform', it was rather consequent that Gunnar Myrdal's thesis should focus on price theory. More specifically the price formation problem and the role of change in this process.[8]

The conventional wisdom maintained that prices were a function of demand and supply, a function basically the same whether the commodity in question was labour, commodities or money. Whenever there was a mismatch it was essentially due to extra-economical factors interfering in the free course of the market mechanism. Most notably the structural unemployment in sectors of the Swedish economy in the 1920's was explained by 'wage stickiness', the fact that the wages were not reduced fast enough to meet actual demand, due to trade union resistance.

Myrdal did not challenge this conventional wisdom head on, instead he reformulated the problem, asking how price levels were developed in the first place. How are changes brought about?

His conclusions severely contradicted Cassel's expectations of a 'purely economic' science, with mathematical precision. To understand the *dynamics* of the market mechanisms Myrdal introduced the central role of the *expectations* held by various economic actors: 'Change, anticipated as a possibility or certainty, enters as one of the primary determining factors'.[9]

Now this was introducing a distinctly subjective element at the heart of the process. This discovery had implications far beyond the area of economics – or of political economy as Myrdal consistently called this science – it also challenged the pretentions of scientific objectivity that this science could maintain – in regard to other sciences.

The science of law had traditionally considered itself as the most prestigious of all social sciences. But in the nineteenth century – as natural scientists were discovering natural laws governing organic life – they came to regard themselves as bearers of unshakeable truths. At the beginning of the twentieth century neo-classical economists came to see themselves much in the same way, and regarded the laws of economy as equally unshakeable. Cassel's approach was based on such a faith in the objectivity of the laws of the economy. There was no need to speculate on what was at the root of value creation in the economy, because value was demonstrated by the choices people made between different kinds of utilities. Prices were a demonstration of values that were inherent in the production. Cassel meant that discarding any discussion on the theory of values, economists should be able to present the theory of prices – upon which any social debate had to build when distinguishing between possibles and impossibles in politics.

Now that Myrdal had shown that the very subjective factors of expectations and anticipation were at the heart of price formation, it was evident there was no such thing as a neutral, objective political economy. The anticipations of the participant actors were evidently a subjective factor introduced into the equation.

In a series of lectures in 1928 Myrdal developed the philosophical conclusions of his work on the price formation problem, and of the role of the 'changeability' in the process. This series was subsequently published in 1930 as *Vetenskap och politik i nationalekonomien*[10] and can be seen as the consequence of Myrdal's investigation on price dynamics, while pushing the reasons behind the failed objectivity of neo-classical economy to its philosophical roots:

Social science is at present living in a time of ruptures. What is needed among other things conclusively and throughout to limit the demands/expectations on the results of this research to what is reasonable from a scientific theoretically point of view. A line between 'what is' and 'what ought to be', between what can be ascertained as true and what should be considered as valuable has to be drawn in full clarity. As long as one still – often without noticing it – mixes up scientific facts with political ideals, theories with ideologies, there will remain a hopeless confusion of opinions even in the most important scientific issues. To no use at all lots of speculative intelligence and dialectical talent will be wasted on fictive problems and battles of words. The strictly scientific findings will be burdened by and hidden under the ideological slag.

Noting that the discussion about political ideas was equally distorted by this lack of separation between scientific facts and ideals he continued:

It is assimilating too much of the mentality that has always been characterizing scientific rationalizations of political dogmas – for instance those of the liberalist political economy in its classic as well as neoclassic versions. This makes room for the same kind of rigid demonstrations of 'evidence' that can be upheld the more stubbornly since they appear to be rational conclusions from self-evident propositions. They show the same kind of predilection for logicistic formulas and axiomatic magic. And during all these awkward intellectual procedures they are succeeding in maintaining the strongest respect for the pure rationality and strictly factual character of their own line of thought.

What then could be done to escape from the prevalent 'predilection for logistic formulas and axiomatic magic'? Characterizing the discussion on political ideas as well as that of economic science as a caricature he stated:

What is needed is to draw a line, from the standpoint of the theory of science, methodically and consequently. It is first of all needed to make scientific research itself free and capable to progress. Anyone who is seeing the matter with a fresh look cannot avoid being bewildered by the ostensibly sterile character still displayed by the research in political economy in some of its most important areas bordering to politics, such as theories on public finance. The cleansing work, motivated by the point of view of theory of science, is however also needed for the economic research to be so oriented that it really serves the political life.

What then were the premises guiding the political economists of the time? With reference to the moral philosophy of the Swedish philosopher Axel Hägerström Myrdal continued:

There are no values in an objective sense, only subjective valuations. These must be differentiated from our perception of reality. This thought is the central starting point for the present critical analysis of economic theory. One thing has to be declared at the outset. It is not enough to maintain that economic research should be value-free and only orient itself towards observation of facts and causal links between facts. Especially now, when economists have become more shy than their classic and neo-classic forerunners openly to present a basic doctrine on objective values, these values are usually hidden and only implicitly understood in the methods of thought used. It is therefore necessary for us to search deeper and attack the normative and teleological ideology of political economy at its foundations.[11]

When first formulated this fundamental critique of the framework of neo-classical economy had the effect of a torch thrown into the sacrosanct church of dominant economists. This challenge also had an aspect of a generational conflict – all those who later were to be part of the so-called Stockholm School of Economists were considerable younger that Cassel, Heckscher and the other more traditional economists.

In a lecture given in 1935, when he took over the chair previously held by his tutor Gustav Cassel, Myrdal argued that crisis and sudden changes of the generally accepted world view influenced research and demonstrated how subjectivity – and values – influenced the researcher.[12] Here he developed his critique against the 'objectivist'pretentions of neo-classic economists and lifted it to a more general level. He started with description of what he called 'the eternal dilemma and innermost tragedy' of research:

> Since the efforts of research have always been and always must be to furnish true knowledge, to be objective, to be unbiased, this actual tie to the assumptions of world and life philosophies contains the eternal dilemma of research and its innermost tragedy, its essential absurdity. In the deepest sense the absurdity lies in the inevitability of the apriority, the unverified and unverifiability even on the theoretical level. It lies in the fact that unfortunately one must ask in order to get an answer and in the fact that the very question constitutes a decision that to a certain degree determines the answer. In other words, the answer is not and cannot be unbiased.'

But then, what of the search for truth in research? How to deal with the inevitability of bias and still try to furnish true knowledge? Myrdal differentiates between two approaches in social sciences, the 'scientifically naïve' method and the 'value-critical' method and gives the following answer:

Apriority is unavoidable, but there are two general methods to bypass the apriority and thereby make the impossible possible. The one method I have already characterized as the epistemologically naïve. It consists of an uncritical acceptance of a certain world image and a certain complex of philosophic ideals.

These are put forth as 'natural,' as conclusions from certain self-evident philosophical principles or from certain elementary psychological sentences that themselves do not have to be substantiated – or they might also (and usually) not be presented at all but are implicitly assumed and incorporated in the methods and results of the research. This naïve method of coming to grips with apriority characterizes, with very few exceptions, the entire past century's economic research and therefore stamps all the liberal economic theory inherited from the prewar period.

The other method, which I would like to call the value critical, can, in my opinion, for certain reasons, be expected to lead to a more fruitful research, at least at times when the social world image rapidly changes. The choice of systematic assumptions – of questions in theoretical research and of value premises in the practical – is then made consciously and becomes clarified by sociological and epistemological analysis. The assumptions are presented as chosen; they are not taken as natural or derived from principle. They are presented exactly and as concretely as possible in the sense that they are placed in relation to factual institutional conditions and human valuations. This method is more honest. From a purely methodical point of view it also has the advantage of not obfuscating fruitful and practically relevant questions, as often happens with the popularly metaphysical superficiality that is inevitable when applying the scientifically naive method.

Once the inevitability of valuations is accepted, then what kind of values are pertinent? Myrdal assumes a close interrelationship between science and society, specifying the criteria of the relevant scientific research:

Quite aside from the question about social causes behind the determination of choices – a socio-psychological problem that will be passed over here – it must be pointed out that epistemological questions and value premises in a social science guided by considerations concerning practical utility must be connected to real conditions and courses of events. It stands to reason that research ought to concern the world that exists. Its theoretical questions should therefore deal with institutional relationships that are real. And even when it comes to the pure value premises within direct practical research, the demand, to my mind, must be made and met, that these value premises should be 'relevant' in the sense that they actually correspond to existing real attitudes and action alternatives of the existing social power groups. Therefore, the conditionality of scientific theory is not arbitrariness.

The criteria of relevance thus meant that research should be guided by practical utility and connected to real events, and that the value premises chosen should not be random but correspond to real attitudes and real action alternatives of the existing social groups. This criteria of relevance showed that his passion lay in social sciences and in socially useful research. Myrdal then presents a paradox – the empirically naive approach is seemingly more objective and neutral, but the value-critical method is a condition for genuine objectivity:

In a strongly dynamic social world the greater awareness of the conditionality in the systematic assumptions is a condition for research to maintain its connection to reality. This is why I uphold the values-critical method's superiority particularly in the current period of development; in an institutionally and politically more stable period, its superiority in this regard would not be so marked.

At the same time – which is more difficult to make comprehensible – it is a condition for genuine objectivity. Through the critical self-reflection of research, issues and value premises first become problematical. In this awareness lies the protection against the otherwise existing danger of unconscious, not scrutinized biases of interests and opinions, that is against a social partiality allegedly self-evident.

I say that this assertion is more difficult to understand. This is because the methodically naïve research, on the contrary, has the appearance of the most absolute objectivity. Its bias is concealed. Since it is unaware of its systematic assumptions, it results in the unconditioned, the seemingly objective policy. By now snatching away the curtain of unconsciousness, the need for questions and value premises is revealed, and the essential conditionality – the absurdity of non-prejudice and complete objectivity – becomes obvious. But thereby and through the critical bias analysis that then appears necessary, what is brought out is the degree or type of objectivity that is reasonable and is achieved by taking the systematic assumptions into account and placing them in relation to real social conditions and human valuations. Social science achieves its objectivity by first discovering the limits to objectivity and then applying scientifically critical methods even when the non-objective is introduced into the analysis and then subsequently accounted for.

Thus the search for truth is possible. Mutual understanding is possible insofar as limits to objectivity are recognized and scientifically critical methods are applied. The recognition of the inescapability of values and biased beliefs does not stand in the way of the search for rational solutions to social problems but it heightens the exigencies of self reflection and transparency in scientific research.

During his whole life Myrdal was struggling with the issues of values, valuations and beliefs in science. Later in his life he felt that his probing of the role of valuations in economics had not gone deep enough in 1930:

> At that time I still thought that there was a valuation-free economic theory and this is evident throughout the book. Now, after having studied in many areas, I know that this conception is wrong and that value premises are necessary in order to scientifically order reality, and establish facts and causal connections between facts.[13]

To find concealed valuations in seemingly factual accounts is an important but difficult task to which Myrdal devoted considerable energy in his subsequent research. On various occasions he demonstrates how concepts such as 'markets', 'free competition', 'welfare', 'unemployment' and 'gross national income' are profoundly value laden. His two major works, *An American Dilemma* (1944) and *Asian Drama* (1968) are thus complemented with ample appendices of methodological discussions aimed at clarifying the scientific process behind the conclusions.

And then there is the effort to clarify his own valuations and beliefs.[14] His own professed valuations are those of the Enlightenment, presented as belief in an optimistic view on the 'perfectability' of human beings, on the values of rationalism and egalitarianism. When discussing the roots of economic theory in 1930 he distinguishes between two theories, the doctrine of harmony and that of utilitarianism which is also labelled as the egalitarian principle. One might also regard this as the difference between economic and political liberalism. Economic liberalism with its faith in the link between individual economic freedom and the common good provided by 'the invisible hand' of the markets[15] and its positivist belief in economic laws on the one hand, and on the other in political liberalism, with its moral emphasis on equality of human rights, where freedom is dependent on the possibility of each individual to actually have access to that equality.

Myrdal also raised the question of relevance of valuations very early on. Valuations applied in research should correspond to existing real attitudes and possible choices for social groups with power. This was truly the case both in his study on race relations in the US and development problems in

South Asia. In the former study the 'American Creed' constituted a moral challenge posed to the ruling elites in their behaviour towards the African American minority. Modernization was an officially declared objective for the Indian ruling party and elites. In both cases his research approach was aimed as a tool for social reform – initiated by the elites.

What then is the importance of Myrdal's value-critical approach to science today? Some parts of this approach might seem self-evident in wider academic circles today. A forceful critique of the positivism that underpinned research in social sciences, most notably in the sphere of economics, has been developed in many quarters in the latter part of the twentieth century: the so-called 'linguistic turn' in social sciences promoted by the works of Michel Foucault, the 'constructivism' in International Relations and the ample field of gender studies have likewise emphasized the biased character of scientific notions.

But this understanding of the role that values play in science still has to reach the domain of dominant economic research. Indeed the change in denomination of the scientific domain of economic theory is in itself revealing: it is now generally termed 'economics' instead of 'political economy', the term most frequently used in the early part of the century. While the term 'political economy' noted the fundamental relationship between economic arguments and political issues 'economics' obscures this connection portraying the area as a neatly delineated science, distinct from social and political spheres of society, just as physics was supposed to treat the area of physical relations quite apart from those of biology and chemistry.

Far from taking heed of the development in other sciences the majority of economists today seem to be satisfied with the actual state of economics, producing more 'scientific results' than ever, all based on fundamentally flawed assumptions.

How are we to understand the persistence of the continued predominance of the convictions of economists in their objectivist models? Myrdal's characterization of the neo-classical economists comes to mind: 'a predilection for logistic formulas and axiomatic magic.'

In 1978 he still harboured a certain hope that this kind of economics would make room for a broader institutional approach in political economy:

> I think that it is predestined to gain terrain in the near future at the expense of conventional economics, but not primarily because of the strength of its logic. Institutionalism will be more predominating since we need a broader approach to handle efficiently with the practical and political problems that are piling up, threatening to drown us. I think that much of the presently established economics, and especially

its most abstract theoretical constructions, which until now have been held in the highest esteem among economists, will be left at the road-side as irrelevant and uninteresting.[16]

This optimism however has not yet been vindicated. On the contrary, neo-liberalism, which can be seen as an extreme form of neo-classical economy, became the dominating economic paradigm at the beginning of the 1980's and has remained so ever since. The conviction that the role of the states had to be rolled back and that of the markets had to be expanded was based on theoretically justified 'inevitabilities'. The statement 'There is No Altern-ative' (TINA) epitomized this attitude. The tenets of neo-classical and neo-liberal economy still form the basis of the curriculum in economics and in economic research despite the fact that the problems then identified by Myrdal (on inequalities, environmental threats and so on) have deepened. Perhaps one of the possible answers to that paradox lies in the prevalence of our perceptions of the present realities that reign over possible futures. Or as Myrdal put it: 'methodically naive research ... has the appearance of the most absolute objectivity. Its bias is concealed. Since it is unaware of its systematic assumptions, it results in the unconditioned, the seemingly objective policy.'

Still there are lively currents of economists working with heterodox ideas.[17] In the wake of the turmoil caused by the first major crises of the liberal globalization wave – the Asian crisis in 1999 and the IT-crash in 2000 – frustration among students and teachers of economics in Paris, London and Harvard resulted in appeals against 'toxic textbooks' and the creation of a network of 'Post-Autistic Economists'. Their demands for theories – and textbooks – more close to real societies, more open to dia-logue is completely in line with Myrdal's approach to scientific work in general and political economy especially.

The economic developments after the financial crisis of 2008 have utterly increased the relevance of Myrdal's demand for a fundamentally changed approach to problems of the political economy.

As Edward Fulbrook, one of the researchers behind the Post-Autistic Economists, recently said:

No discipline has ever experienced systemic failure on the scale that economics has today. Its fall from grace has been two-dimensional. One, economists oversaw, directly and through the prevalence of their ideas, the structuring of the global economy that has now collapsed. Two, except for a few outcasts, economists failed to see, even before the general public saw, the coming of the biggest economic meltdown of all time. Never has a profession betrayed the trust of society so acutely, never has one been in such desperate need of a fundamental remake.

As an epistemological event, the 2008 meltdown of the global financial system ranks with the observation of the 1919 solar eclipse. If professional practice in economics resembled, even in the slightest, that in the natural sciences, then in the wake of today's global disaster economists would be falling over each other to proclaim the falsity of their theories, the inadequacy of their methods and the urgent need for new ones.[18]

In the present situation Myrdal's basic tenets concerning scientific approach are consequently more relevant than ever. His value-critical method, insisting on the inevitability of values and valuations in research is something that has to be re-asserted as the basis for any scientific debate on equal terms. There are no answers without questions, there are no views without viewpoints. Those questions are inevitably based on valuations, subjective biases, prejudices or not. The viewpoint is determining the light shed on the specific problem under scrutiny. This entails an obligation to scrutinize the open and the hidden assumptions, and to evaluate the general applicability and depth of the conclusions presented. In that respect Myrdal's value-critical approach is shared by large numbers of heterodox economists and social scientists. But beyond this consciously critical attitude, I think Myrdal's scrupulous efforts at making his own value premises explicit and transparent, merits reflection. This side of his value-critical method is much less followed since it makes the personal biases and beliefs of researchers more open to critique. It is a much safer position to hide one's driving passions and predilections behind the armour of theories and well articulated criticisms than to lay open the limits of one's objectivity. I think this courage should be valued, since it adds a democratic dimension to the discussion because the researcher is no longer the expert conducting a battle on a scene but a participant in search of a common good. The self-reflective aspect of Myrdal's approach to science will no doubt enrich the individual researcher's work, and make her/him differentiate between the values, beliefs and prejudices that are underlying their work.

By making the individual researcher more visible it will also strengthen the relation between research and society, it will make the 'scientific community' more open to citizen scrutiny.

The question of time in neo-classical economics

We have seen how Myrdal's dissertation on economics developed into a fundamental questioning of the methodological and philosophical foundations of political economy. Now we shall turn to how he developed his critical questions within the parameters given by economic theory itself.

Originally Myrdal had a modest purpose with his dissertation in 1927. It was only 'to introduce, to some degree, the variability factor to the study of price formation, i.e. to liberate it from its static prerequisite'.[19]

As he started his investigation the idea of equilibrium in the economy was something he had fundamental doubts about:

> The assumption that there is a state of equilibrium towards which the current price formation tends – that there is for every product, service, or means of production a certain price that is, in this purely technical sense, 'natural' or 'normal' in relation to those currently valid – is actually as old as economic theory itself. Theoretical analysis is nothing but a study of such states of equilibrium and their conditions, plus the causes that prevent their continual realization.[20]

He granted that the approximation of assuming all price factors to be constant and equally changing might be a good and often a sufficient approximation of the real situation. But when he was trying to understand the actual price formation process he was brought further and further away from this hypothesis of 'static' conditions.

Even if the mere simplicity of the 'static explanation' was useful, since it allowed for the introduction of several supplementary conditions, the pretentions of portraying these simplified static constructions as 'normal' or 'natural' in regard to reality was a truth with great modification:

> But price formation occurs in the human psyche. This is why notions about future changes as more or less probable and the wider evaluations about the degree of uncertainty in these notions are factors influencing the current price-formation process.[21]

This understanding of the price formation process as a mental process was undoubtedly new. It was in fact a fundamental refutation of the neoclassical economy's pretention of having established an objective, neutral ground for economic theory.

But Myrdal also raised another question that dealt a further blow to the static equilibrium hypothesis. He called into question the conventional economists' complete lack of interest in the question of time lags. In neoclassical theory all production factors are supposed to be instantly reacting to changes in output and demand, thus finding new optimal equilibriums. But while this 'static approximation of an atomistic price formation may often be a useful, even necessary approximation, what is erroneous is only the assertion that the atomistic price formation would in an economic sense be normal in regard to the real.'[22]

In real life, where price formation actually took place, he found that this was never the case:'The economic inertia of the means of production is now of such an extraordinary importance that it must be unthinkable and inadmissible to make abstraction from this in the general dynamic problem of equilibrium.'[23]With this introduction of the relative weight or inertia – or 'stickiness' as it is sometimes called – the question of time in the adaptation process was added.

Not only was public opinion in all its variety a constitutive factor in determining prices but moreover, social and material conditions involved had to be taken into account. The question of inertia in all the complexity of industrial organization, worker mobility and social conditions entered into the picture.

In real life price formation did not occur in total flexibility. Stickiness and the component of risk were thus very important components shaping the process.

As noted in the previously this fundamentally undermined the pretentions of economic theorists to be able to produce precise scientific knowledge on how prices were determined.

From a modest beginning the conclusions of Myrdal's 1927 dissertation made him move ever further away from the equilibrium analysis. In 1929–1930 he was staying in New York on research leave – and having witnessed the onslaught of the Wall Street Crash he started to reflect on the dynamics behind this crash and on monetary theory in general. In doing so he radically changed his starting point: it was by exploring the concepts of another Swedish economist, Knut Wicksell, that he tried to capture the dynamics of the economy. The answer he found made him take a further step in his analysis regarding the consequences of introducing the time dimension into the price formation process.

In 1928 he saw political economy stemming from a double heritage, with inherent tensions. On the one hand the idea of 'law of nature' – with its connections to the understandings of the 'laws of nature' in the physical world – and on the other the philosophy of utilitarianism. He termed this difference as one between '*harmonitanken*' (the idea of harmony) and '*likhetstanken*' (the idea of equality). It was this idea of harmony that reflected itself in the firm belief of neo-classical economists in the immanent laws of the economy as tending towards equilibrium. By choosing to explore monetary theory in the footsteps of Knut Wicksell he entered a completely different line of reasoning: that of dynamic causation.

Knut Wicksell, a self-taught, but gifted unorthodox economist, is generally considered to be one of Sweden's most influential early economists. He had developed his theories out of demographic studies. In monetary matters Wicksell was above all concerned with understanding how cumulative chains developed. He maintained that there was a natural rate of interest, determined by tangible factors in the economy such as the productivity of capital and the cost of production. He saw this as opposed to the market rate of interest determined by financial institutions that had the discretionary capability of emitting credits and creating money. According to Wicksell there was by no means a necessary convergence between the two rates of interest. Rather it accrued to public authorities to control the financial markets in such a way that market interests did not exceed the natural rate of interest – in which case there might be a cumulative tendency towards depression.[24] In a series of lectures in 1931 on Wicksell's monetary theory,[25] Myrdal made what he termed as an 'immanent analysis' of this theory. By 'immanent analysis' Myrdal meant an analysis probing the inner consistency of Wicksell's theory, following its assumptions and then drawing his own conclusions. To quote one of the reviewers of *Monetary Equilibrium* (1939), Myrdal had 'developed how Wicksell should have thought if he had thought logically correct'.

Myrdal asked what would happen when what people perceive as the 'natural' interest rate is higher than the current money rate of interest. Credit would be perceived as cheap, profit expectations high – businesses would be stimulated to borrow and spend on capital formation. This might further stimulate upward pressure on prices. The ultimate result would be highly dependent on expectations and on how those expectations had developed.

Wicksell had argued that price stability could be regarded as criteria of monetary equilibrium. But this was by no means evident from Wicksell's own theory, according to Myrdal: 'A theoretical construction far from clarified seems to be correct because it is "practical", a valuation becomes a truth, a quite old experience from the history of economic doctrines.'[26] Price stability was in fact something that only could be established by analysing past events while the dynamics of prices were largely determined by anticipation. What Myrdal called 'the dynamic price formation problem' was in fact raising two problems of a completely different nature, problems that it was necessary and urgent to distinguish between:

> The one problem is how one price-formation position changes into another. The question here deals with the causal effects *in future time* of currently occurring changes. However, these changes also have effects *backwards in time*; this is because they are anticipated. The latter problem is the primary one theoretically. For it is the price-formation situation, in which anticipations have been co-determinate, that is hit by the changes, and thereby develops into a new one. In other words, a study of the former problem requires solution of the latter one.[27]

In understanding this we already have the premises of the necessity of the *ex ante/ex post* – distinction in economic analysis. That is, the need to differentiate between the *ex ante* analysis discussing the possible outcomes of different policies given a particular set of conditions, and the *ex post* analysis where outcomes are known and the task is to understand the causation by taking all relevant factors into account. This notion of the *ex ante/ ex post* distinction was in fact for the first time explicitly presented in the German version of Myrdal's treatise on monetary theory. In the English version of this treatise Myrdal regarded this as 'probably the chief contribution of this essay'.[28]

In the preceding section we explored Myrdal's critique of the 'objectivist'pretentions of neo-classical economics. Myrdal's argument on monetary theory brings us to a second fundamental aspect of his critique of neo-classical economics: its lack of the time dimension.

Economists steeped in the neo-classical tradition readily agree the assumption of total flexibility of adjustments to the market mechanism is at best an ideal, and rarely a true representation of realities. They argue, however, that it is a useful approximation, and they often try to introduce estimated time lags and 'stickynesses' to correct the outcome predicted by equilibrium models. However, Myrdal would argue that the time factor should not be introduced as a correction, but should necessarily be at the heart of the analysis.

This was in fact one of his main critical points against the analysis of two other contemporary economists, John Maynard Keynes and Friedrich Hayek that he developed in the English edition of his treatise on monetary theory:

> A criticism of Keynes and Hayek would have to begin by pointing out that in their theoretical systems there is no place for the uncertainty factor and for anticipations. This objection is quite decisive since – as Keynes remarked several times in the applied part of his work though not in the theoretical statement of the problem – the whole monetary problem depends on the factor of adaptation.[29]

Myrdal's emphasis on the role of expectations and risk analysis made room for greater realism but at the same time made the analysis more complicated. Analysing events and chains of reactions historically – *ex post* – would be possible by basically referring to relevant data at hand, constructing more or less convincing explanations. Even if even this exercise had to be done judiciously: '"Facts" are by no means easily palpable things. Especially if they are of a rather general and complex character. Behind each formulation of "facts" are extensive theoretical hypotheses.'[30]

Predicting future developments however was a quite different matter – much more indeterminate – where anticipations of several different actors had to be taken into account.

This distinction between analyses *ex post* and arguments *ex ante* is in fact a fundamental distinction often poorly understood. They represent different types of explanations and pursue different objectives. Ex-post analyses are oriented towards explaining patterns, understanding historical trajectories. Ex-ante analyses on the other hand are more concerned with predicting outcomes, and consequently more policy oriented. To what extent are these components of Myrdal's early contribution to economic theory – the time dimension, the role of anticipations and the distinction between ex post and ex ante – of relevance today?

Initially one may note that the latter distinction has generally been poorly understood by economists. The desire to be able to predict the future – and thus to influence it – has always been strong among economists of the conventional neo-classical mould. While acknowledging the importance of time lags, of inertia and of the psychological element in the behaviour of different actors, great efforts have been invested in trying to gulf the bridge between *ex post* and *ex ante* – with advanced mathematical models of probabilities and estimates of the relative weight of attitudes.

However – on this point the fundamental critique of Myrdal remains valid: there are no fixed laws in the economy. The future cannot be deduced from past events. Myrdal's point that the dynamics of economy must to a large extent be regarded as being a mental process, and the fact that expectations have an impact on the results, is obviously still valid today. Myrdal's early reminders of these fundamental flaws of mainstream neoclassical economic theory have shown themselves to be glaringly acute in the aftermath of the global financial crisis of 2008.

This was very well illustrated by the inability of the majority of professional economists to anticipate the meltdown of the global finance system in 2008. Even Alan Greenspan, the head of US Federal Reserve and venerated as an omniscient guru acknowledged to being stunned by what he called a 'once in a century event'. One may also quote the completely misplaced growth projections produced by the IMF and other international institutions prior to that crisis. They consistently based their projections on previous growth patterns, not accounting for the possibility of real turnabouts. Even in their October 2008 report – at the very moment the crash was unwinding the tissue of global finance – they were projecting continued global growth, even if be it at a lesser scale.

And these prognoses were made with the help of armies of statisticians, built up by databases of the World Bank, the US Federal Reserve, the

Eurostat and the WTO. So it was not because of lack of empirical information that their predictions turned out to be so erroneous. What are we to deduce from such a massive failure? Of course it is not a failure to make a wrong guess. But if a guess is presented as something more reliable, not only an educated guess but a probable outcome it is clearly an abuse of confidence, especially if the economic policies of the world are built on those guesses. It is indeed persisting in the 'scientifically naive' method that Myrdal so often criticized.

And if the actual outcome is not even within the range of projected scenarios, then the flaw is still deeper, as we are witnessing a lack of imagination, a lack of openness to the unpredictability of human conditions. A lack of openness, many have argued, is not coincidental but related to the 'theological' function of present economic elites. Joseph Stiglitz, who as chief economist at the World Bank saw this clergy and its way of functioning from the inside, was deeply critical. He has afterwards amply explained the reasons behind the continuing force of the established doctrines of neo-classical economic theory in this neo-liberal variant, which is also called the 'Washington Consensus'.[31]

The most important factor worth mentioning here is Myrdal's early argument about the danger of using abstract models when analysing economies. Models can be very useful to produce clear-cut results, but what of their quality? The first task must be to establish a starting point that gives a relevant picture of the multifaceted character of the social and economic spheres, whose reactions are to be analysed. During a long – too long – period, perhaps by colonial deference, the public opinion have accepted that envoys of the World Bank were sent to developing 'Third World' countries struggling with debt repayments as almighty experts.[32] After a couple weeks they were often ready to offer political prescriptions, devoid of any deep knowledge of the country they were visiting. When – at the present moment – the same kind of economists are issuing clearly counter-productive – not to say nonsensical – directives to countries in the European Union, it should be obvious that their map has taken precedence over real geography.

The second important lesson to be drawn here from Myrdal is the need to make a thorough distinction between *ex post* and *ex ante*. It is important to distinguish between analyses trying to understand specific historic sequences of events, and discussions on how to facilitate or avoid certain future scenarios. This distinction must be made much more explicit in the general economical debate. The whole elaboration of the prognosis machinery of the IMF, WTO and their affiliated agencies is designed to blur this distinction, to make the general public accept their projections as realities, thereby closing the arena of democratic debates. What must be resisted is not making prognoses as such, but their pretentions of being able to make reliable predictions, of describing future certainties.

Third the 'risk point of view' evoked by Myrdal has to be understood in its very fundamental and incalculable dimension. The danger of modelling 'insecurity' into the economy has been eloquently demonstrated by the building up of the global financial crisis. Notably by the profusion of 'financial instruments' in the sub-prime sector of the US mortgage markets. The risk involved in any financial commitment was in fact converted into still another source of profit. By 'trading away' risky engagements in the housing sector with the aid of derivatives, mortgage-lending institutions thought they had cleared the way for another round of profit-making mortgage lending. By acquiring interest yielding assets in the form of credit derivatives, intermediate financial institutions felt certain to reap steady financial profits. And as the leading theorists assured: the wider the risk was shared, the lower the probability of miscalculation. As the British economist Roberty Skidelsky has shown, all these economic models were based on assumptions of 'efficiently functioning financial markets' and probability curves of a 'normal' Gaussian distribution.[33] In his much discussed book *The Black Swan* the epistemologist Nassim Taleb argued the importance of events totally outside probability estimates, highly improbable events with far-reaching consequences.[34]

Future developments cannot be deduced from history – however broadly collected the 'facts'. This doesn't mean that historical analogies are useless, on the contrary, they provide a fertile basis for discussions about possible futures. In the latter discussions it is the qualities of imagination and broad social knowledge that are most relevant, and not computing diagrams. It is this fundamental difference between historical analysis and prediction that is lost in the predominating modelling efforts, developed by the armies of economists trained in the econometrics of neoclassical theories. To this critique against the assumed 'normal distribution' of probabilities must be added another aspect of the time dimension: its cumulative and irreversible character. Within a stable framework of institutions and parameters comparison between patterns of economic fluctuations can be valuable, but what value can such comparisons have when parameters are fundamentally different? Actual models compiled by the main international institution are based on the patterns of business cycles in the preceding decades. But the dimensions of the financial crisis in 2008 surpassed all the downturns of these cycles, the scale of the economies involved were much wider, the downturn afterwards was much sharper. How then could such models be useful tools for prognoses?

When the neo-liberal economists are applying probability curves in analysing economic tendencies they fail to understand the difference between probability and insecurity. The former can be deduced *ex post*, the latter establishes the definite limits of the validity of any prognosis. That is something they could have learnt by reading Gunnar Myrdal.

The basic tendency of markets: equilibrium or dynamics?

There is yet another line of Myrdal's argumentduring the thirties that needs to be explored and that is whether there is a basic movement inherent in market economies?

In his study on the price formation problem Myrdal was moving away from the equilibrium analysis as a useful departing point. Gradually he reached a more realistic analysis of the nature of economic processes by introducing the central role of expectations. And with the treatise on monetary theory 1931 he took a further step towards a theory of the dynamics in the economy. Myrdal started with an investigation of the monetary theory of Knut Wicksell. How was a stable price level to be established? In Wicksell's view a stable price level was an indication of a monetary equilibrium. What kind of monetary policy did it require? In pursuing the dynamic approach of Wicksell Myrdal adopted the view, that price developments were basically a 'cumulative process'. Myrdal asked himself, what would happen, according to Wicksell's theory, if there was a dynamic deviation in one direction or the other from a monetary equilibrium?

His analysis of the way Wicksell presented the different conditions necessary for equilibrium in monetary policy, made Myrdal refute the whole idea of a 'normal' rate of interest that would be able to secure price stability and a balance between investments and savings. That such a 'normal' rate would emerge out of the relation between 'net income' and the reproduction costs of real capital was by no means logically given. Both these terms depended on anticipations of different agents in the economy. Even the proposition that a stable price level would represent a monetary equilibrium with a 'normal' interest rate was discarded by Myrdal. It was by no means logically necessary, he meant: 'A construction that is far from evident principally appears to be true since it seems to be "practical", thus a valuation is presented as a truth, which is in fact an old experience from the history of economic doctrines.'[35]

Even when a stable price level existed it was not self-evident that this would correspond to a 'normal' interest rate – nor to any equality between savings and investments. As Myrdal explained, the idea that a stable price could represent a 'centre of gravity' for actual price movements was not even argued by Wicksell: 'The thought developed is on the contrary that non-equilibrium initiates a movement away from equilibrium. That is in fact why the movement becomes cumulative.'[36]

Another important point made in this essay on monetary theory was that monetary equilibrium – in the sense of an equality between *ex ante* savings and investments – could be established at very different price and interest levels. Even more important – it was evident that when equality between *ex ante* savings and *ex ante* investments occurred this would coincide with a state of maximum employment, as neo-classical economists maintained.[37]

What then could be the reach of monetary policy? Myrdal argued that discount rate policies have a very limited reach, because of the numerous impediments to market reactions to such changes ('stickyness' of wage rates, stabilized consumption patterns, market power of firms). His conclusion was that monetary policies had to be related into a larger framework if the aim was to maintain a high level of production and employment:'Maintaining a monetary equilibrium becomes a question not only of monetary policy but of economic policy as a whole, social policy and the institutions which rule the labour market, cartel legislation and all related factors.'[38]As noted earlier the inquiry on monetary theory and the role of money in the economy brought Myrdal into a fundamentally dynamic conception of 'causation' in economics. Not only did he refute the neo-classical claim that there was tendency towards a 'natural' equilibrium in the economy, assuming full mobility of production factors. He was not alone in doing so. But he also went beyond one of Keynes' main ideas in his *General Theory*, the possibility of several different levels of equilibrium. He argued that the basic tendency in the economy was rather dynamic movements away from equilibrium however defined.

This made him argue the paramount importance of political intervention to counter mounting imbalances. In his analysis he showed that 'price stability' was in no way an evidence of equilibrium, but a value, and consequently something that had to be scrutinized from an ideological point of view. Another important point to note in Myrdal's analysis of monetary theory was his insistence, that monetary policy had to be developed within the larger framework of economic and social policy as a whole. That was necessary since it had to be based not on 'objective' facts or 'natural rates' but on values and desires, once the metaphysics of equilibrium tendencies had been removed.

The full impact of Myrdal's journey in and out of Wicksell's dynamic approach wasn't obvious until his 1931 essay was translated into English in 1939. But by then the publication of Keynes' *General Theory* had already changed the intellectual landscape of economic theory. The publication of *Monetary Equilibrium* is for that reason generally read in the light of Keynes' work, which might be somewhat unfair. Without falling into the trap of 'who was first' – intellectual processes are largely social with parallel movements – it is interesting to note some differences between the two works. Keynes is preoccupied with formulating the conditions for the creation of economic equilibrium with an optimal optimum use of productive forces and employment. Keynes' presentation of the 'liquidity trap' as a constitutive feature of the actual economic crisis, and the multiplicator effect of public policies aimed at raising levels of general demand, are theories that are absent in Myrdal's analysis. Myrdal's ambition in *Monetary Equilibrium* is a different one: understanding the dynamics at hand in the monetary field of economy. He discarded the notion of equilibrium tendencies in the economy, a notion that Keynes still embraced, although he was enlarging it. Myrdal's emphasis in the essay on the dynamic and cumulative tendencies away from 'equilibria' in the economy makes him stress the primordial role of political intervention still more than Keynes does.

There are also quite different conclusions inherent in the two works: where Keynes' policy recommendations still are formulated within the sphere of economics (management of aggregate demand), Myrdal – with his more social analysis of market conditions – is already moving out of the realm of strictly economic theory. He is instead arguing for monetary policies to be integrated in a larger framework of economic and social policy.

Myrdal's analysis of the cumulative dynamics in the economy is only at its beginning in *Monetary Equilibrium*. As we shall see later it was considerably expanded in his social studies and in his analyses of the mechanisms in the international economy.

What then is to be retained from his analysis of the basically cumulative and dynamic tendency of markets today? Evidently the phenomenal and seemingly limitless expansion of the financial economy both nationally and internationally comes to mind. To give just one example: the development of internationally traded derivatives. When the 'Bretton Woods System' of currency relations – relatively regulated arrangement of semi-stable currencies with a US-dollar as anchor pegged to a fixed gold rate – was abandoned in 1970 a fluctuation of rates ensued between the major currencies. As a consequence internationally trading companies needed to secure the values of their long term commercial relations. A financial market for currency assurances (options, term contracts, swaps) evolved. In 1986 the Bank for International Settlements estimated the notional amount of derivatives outstanding to be US$1.088 billion. Some 20 years later it amounted to US$37.660 billion, thus largely exceeding the calculated amount of the world's GDP that year.[39] Ten years later on the equivalent figure recorded by the BIS was US$680.290 billion, dwarfing global GDP more than ten times.[40] Without entering into detail this is a telling illustration of the dynamic tendencies of financial markets away from equilibrium levels. Of course dynamics differ, specific markets have different tendencies. Consumer markets concerned with daily necessities can be expected to be less volatile than currency derivatives. Notably this point has been made by the late Hyman Minsky in his works on the volatility of financial markets.[41] He argued that financial markets were fundamentally unstable, that the dynamic forces of the capitalist economy were explosive and had to be contained by institutional regulations. The far-sightedness of his analysis can hardly be doubted – some six financial crises later.

A further aspect to reflect on about the ideas developed by Myrdal in *Monetary Equilibrium* is his insistence on the need to integrate monetary policies into a larger framework. He emphasized the valuation character of price stability as an aim for monetary policy. In the European Union the constitutionalization of the 'independency' of the Central Banks, and the establishment of 'price stability' as their sole task, is in fact expressing a very value-biased, ideological choice – despite its appeareance of consensuality. By affirming that price stability is its only priority, these central institutions are in fact asserting that full employment is a less important aim, something that in the best of cases might be the result of their 'sound' monetary policies. By defining price stability narrowly on the Consumer Price Index and wages, while ignoring price developments on Stock Markets and in the Equity Markets, they have in fact encouraged a massive redistribution of wealth from wage-earners to the propertied classes.

The role of the public sector in the economy

The dramatic economic events in 1929–1931 were of course the evident backdrop to Myrdal's refutation of neo-classic economic theory and the faith in equilibrium economics as the natural and optimal order of things in economy. The dramatic crashes and the human tragedies caused by impoverishment and unemployment were all too obvious. The larger crisis also took its toll on Sweden. The chain reaction of financial crises unleashed by the bankruptcy of the Austrian *Credit-Anstalt* in May 1931, and the devaluation of the British Pound in September the same year, forced Sweden to leave the Gold Standard. Moreover Sweden had to devalue its currency to restore current balances and introduce regulations on capital movements, in order to protect the economy against speculative flows. Despite these moves – and primarily due to the general slowdown of international trade – Swedish unemployment rose rapidly, to exceed 20 per cent in the wake of Swedish election in 1932.

Given this background, and bearing in mind Myrdal's notion of the dynamics of economy, the questions of economic policy and public finance necessarily came to the fore. If there was no tendency towards equilibrium – how would it be possible to avoid cumulative developments towards depression? What could public authorities do?

During the crisis in 1931 Myrdal published not only the essay on monetary issues, but also an analysis of the effects of the currency crisis on the Swedish economy.[42] He was already regarded as one of the foremost of Sweden's economists. He was also one of the few who publicly supported the Social Democratic government that was elected in 1932. It is illustrative of his position that – although without any formal task in the newly formed government – he was called by the Minister of Finance to write both the introductory economic analysis in the Government Bill for 1933 and – in an appendix to the same bill – a theoretical explanation of the motives behind deficit spending in times of economic contraction.[43]

In the neo-classical view of economy at the time, the State was regarded as somewhat of an anomaly, something foreign to the natural order of things. It was recognized to have a function in maintaining order and tranquillity, a function for which citizens must be prepared to suffer a certain cost by taxation. The ideal of neo-classical economists at the time of Myrdal, was the 'minimal state', sometimes referred to as the 'night-watch state', that is a state securing the sleep of the good people but infringing as little as possible on the dealings of the market economy.

This attitude was also reflected in the deliberations in the different parliaments. When discussing matters of public expenditures and revenue a strictly book-keeping attitude was applied. Balance sheets had to add up, expenditures were being decided annually and they had to adapt to foreseeable receipts. The yearly balancing of the books was seen as a sacrosanct principle of good housekeeping. The public finance thus had a largely passive role, adapting to changing circumstances in the 'real world', the market economy. When receipts were falling due to downturns in the economy restrictions in expenditures were called for as a measure of responsibility.

The ineptitude of these views was exposed clearly as the economic crisis hit Sweden fully in 1931–1932. Receipts were dwindling, due to the general slowdown, and the number of people in distress was steadily mounting. The absurdity of restricting the public sector efforts at a time of vastly increased social needs was indeed a recurrent theme of the Social Democratic Party in the elections in 1932. 'Can we afford to work?' was the title of a pamphlet produced in the Social Democratic campaign, written by Ernst Wigforss.

But once in power the Social Democratic government lacked the theoretical arguments for such an attitude. The arguments were presented by Myrdal in the form of the appendix mentioned above. This much celebrated report by Myrdal amounted to a breach with the neo-classical passive view on the public finance in several ways. Moreover it produced the theoretical argument for an active, counter-cyclical role of the public sector. Myrdal restated the problem as being not the soundness of public finances. The major problem was the effects of public finance on the economy as a whole:

> Given the size of the public economic activities it is evident that the volume, the orientation and financing of these activities ... will exert a substantial influence on the economic development in the country. Primarily the problem is how the state should orient its financial policy so that it at least will not unnecessarily aggravate the current depression thereby increasing unemployment.[44]

A limited aim it may seem: but at the same time it was above all – by subordinating accounting principles to the more general discussion of the effects of public policies on economy as a whole – that the order of priorities was changed. Counteracting depression and unemployment was the overall objective, and principles had to be arranged accordingly.

Myrdal analysed the problem from two points of view: that of public finances and that of conjunctural and social policy concerns. Financially, he argued, that the costs of expansion of public activities on projects of infrastructure were vastly overrated. Such projects would in general be less costly in times of depression, it was only the irrationality of the annual accounting system that made them look costly.

One of the driving forces in the development of depression was the strong pessimism among businessmen, in itself a factor that was lessening revenues and increasing public costs. A public policy working against such pessimism would entail a lessening of public costs. To that should be added the overall value created by the expansion of public works, and the revenues that could be estimated as a result of the stimulus given to business and the reduction of unemployment. As a conclusion, Myrdal argued: 'If one adopts a financial viewpoint on the problem with full consequence and in a somewhat longer time frame this viewpoint does not stand in conflict with concerns of conjunctural and social policies, rather it is widely supporting them.'[45]

When analysing the problem from the social viewpoint he claimed that the cost of increased government expenditures was no cost at all, once one took into account the effects of prolonged unemployment ('lowering the nation's "personal" capital, that is the future productive capacity of the unemployed and of their families') and the positive value created in public works. From the social viewpoint 'it is evident that such an expansion of the public activities is even more "profitable" than it has shown to be from the viewpoint of public finances".[46]

This argument was further strengthened: 'To this comes the fact that the real burdens of unemployment are falling especially heavily on the classes in society that are less well off. The social policy view is thus forcefully emphasizing this conclusion.'

Myrdal argued that this expansion of public works should not be financed by raising taxes, since this would hamper general demand which would be strengthen depression. Instead it should be financed by public borrowing. But wouldn't this have the effect of crowding out the access of private investors? He was keen to allay those fears, arguing that in the actual situation of depression there was a reluctance to invest and a lot of real capital was under-employed, especially in sectors that would benefit from the expansion of public works. Second, increased savings in society as a whole as a consequence of increased incomes would provide for the credits needed: 'From the view point of the capital markets there is thus no reason why the government should fail to take this initiative that the private businessmen hesitate to do.'[47]

In his conclusion he notes, that even if the actual system gives some lee-way in stretching the principles of annual balances by shifting between different capital accounts, he recommends a reform of the accounting system, sidelining the annual accounting restrictions by creating a separate 'counter-cyclic fund'. He argued that a strict differentiation should be established between current expenditures on the one hand and capital investments on the other, the latter being financed by a 'pluriannual finance plan for public works.'

There are several points of Myrdal's methodology to be noted here. First: replacing the problem in question into a wider framework. The problem of public finances is not an accounting problem but part of a wider social and economic problem of how to handle the depression in a socially and economically rational way?

Second, he starts by accepting the premises of his hidden, conservative opponents, presenting it as a dilemma that can be transcended. Yes, their reticence against increased taxes is justified and the fear among political and economic elites of increased expenditures is acknowledged. Then he shows that, when considering alternative costs, expansion of public works might be a cheap way out even for business interests, especially when also considering new income opportunities. Present also is Myrdal's insistence on the role of anticipation. It is the task of public authorities to counter undue pessimism, to counter a 'waste of the productive forces of the country'. Moreover there is his conviction that, although expressing himself from a Social Democratic platform, what he outlined was something of defending general interest, something favourable for businessmen as well as workers.

This report was thus included in the official version of the first Government Bill of the newly elected Social Democratic government. It was followed by political measures to a very limited extent. Public works expanded in 1932–1933 but were already restricted in 1934 despite an unemployment level of 18 per cent. In fact – in only three out of the eight pre-war years did the Social Democratic government pursue an expansive financial policy.[48]

What then of Myrdal's proposals for an overhaul of the accounting system? Not even on this account was he much luckier. The need to establish new rules for budget policies was widely recognized, and in 1936 parliamentary commission of 'Budgetsakkunniga' (Experts on Budgetary matters) was set up and Myrdal played an active role. He managed to convince conservative economists (Cassel and Hildebrand) of the necessity of introducing a separate 'Konjunkturutjämningsfond' (Fund for equalization of business cycles) to enable a more smoothly working countercyclical economic policy. But it was definitely more difficult for Myrdal to convince his fellow Social Democrats in the government of such a turn towards a more active economic policy. The stumbling block was the conservatism of the Minister of Finance Ernst Wigforss, and of his deputy Dag Hammarskjöld.[49] The proposals of the commission were watered down to a symbolic change of name. 'Kassafonden' (the Cash Fund) which changed its name to 'Budgetutjämningsfonden' (the Budget Equalization Fund) – was allotted the task of equalizing budget imbalances – and was given an amount which was totally inadequate for the task of equalizing business cycles.[50]

When Myrdal addressed an American audience on the principles of counter-cyclical fiscal policies in 1939, it was as a consequence with the backdrop of a rather disappointing political experience. He started by acknowledging his bewilderment about

> the irrational complexity of our budgetary systems due to attempts to present balanced budgets even when they are not balanced. ... It is this play with ficticious economies, branched out into all items of the budget to conceal an actual deficit from the general public and sometimes, also, from the legislators, which makes an economist feel so hopeless in dealing with budgetary matters.[51]

The topic of his contribution was to discuss how to reconstruct the budget system. But at the outset he noted how 'half-heartedly' the execution of the new, deliberate fiscal deficit policy had been so far:

The depression following the crisis of 1929 turned out to be so serious that even in the most respectable fiscal households the deficits could not be concealed by budgetary tricks of the traditional type. Furthermore, during this depression an almost worldwide deliberate fiscal deficit policy, motivated by the effects on the business situation has been proposed and to some extent put in effect. In most countries, including Sweden (which has served as the laboratory in working out certain of the conclusions which I shall present at a later stage of this paper) this policy was carried out only half-heartedly. Public works were generally begun too late; they were not prepared in advance and were for this reason delayed and scarcely aimed at the works which should have been selected before all others if a rational choice had been made. They were also usually of a much smaller scope than would have been desirable.

The shortcomings of the new policy 'are to a considerable extent to be explained by the fact that this policy was frustrated as a result of being pressed upon a budgetary system which had been built upon a budgetary system contradictory to this self-same policy.'

He concluded that, even if the will to adapt to new circumstances was present, the mere construction of the budgetary system was an obstacle to an appropriate economic policy:

> It is therefore just at present an important problem of economic engineering to construct a new scheme of legal and institutional regulations for fiscal households: a set of fiscal formulas which at the same time guarantees to a satisfactory degree the financial 'soundness' of public finances in the long run and allows enough flexibility from year to year for fiscal policy to serve its purpose of among other measures to mitigate the fluctuations in business activity.[52]

According to Myrdal financial soundness and flexibility were the two complementary aims of fiscal policy. He urged that a thorough distinction should be made between those expenditures that were 'running costs' and those that could be considered as 'investments'. There was in fact no reason why they should be added together: 'an entrepreneur or an individual family would never think of adding together its corresponding accounts'. It was on the latter point that the "soundness" – always put inside quotation marks by Myrdal – of public finance could be measured.

As for financial soundness it was a matter of the development in the long run, and it was basically a political choice:

The trend of the net aggregate value of these assets minus public debts is, then, the measure of the relative soundness of a fiscal system; if this trend is lowered, the finance is somewhat less sound, and vice versa. The degree of "soundness" to be kept up in a system of public finances being the basic principle of fiscal policy, it must be established by a political decision.

The two types of accounts should be financed in different ways. The principle behind the capital investment account was to finance 'profitable, self-liquidating investments' out of loans. What could be considered to be reasonable investments of that character was still however a rather moot point. Myrdal noted that not only public buildings but also the social housing programme was gradually transferred into that category in Sweden and he argued that the entire upkeep and construction of roads should also be accounted as investments. Still, he noted, 'this account will nevertheless be relatively small. There is therefore need for still more flexibility'.

In general, fiscal policy was 'a rather clumsy instrument in crisis policy.... The most we can righteously request from fiscal policy that it shall in a general and rigid way be adjusted to react contrary to cyclical movements.'

This however presupposed a change in mental attitudes:

> If we want public finance to react as a countercycle we must change the political psychology and give the state plenty of resources in depression, but hold them back in booms. Such a change in psychology can be carried out by appropriate alterations in the institutional setup.

He claimed that the newly established Swedish 'Budget equalization fund' was a step in the right direction since it was to operate on a five-year amortization scheme. The fact that this fund was initially of such limited proportions was no obstacle:

> The ordinary maximum height of the equalization fund in a boom is fixed at only 75 million kronor, which means that the normal height over a period of years will be very much under zero. Of course, in the Swedish financial situation in which the state has a capital wealth much in excess of the total national debt, there should have been no difficulty at all in starting the new system by creating a considerable positive fund. When we have chosen, on the contrary, to work with underbalances from bad years to be repaid during good years as the normal course of events, we have followed the pattern of the last

depression. We have thought this to be more advantageous, as there is then no limit to underbalancing during bad years.[53]

Myrdal hoped that this new Swedish system would make it 'possible in the next depression to carry out a much bolder expansionist programme without breaking the established budgetary principles'. Large increases in investments would then be financed by loans and there would be no need to raise taxes with the use of the budget equalizing fund.

He had however a final reservation:

> Finally the point might be raised against this structure of fiscal reaction to various fluctuations that it assumes normal business cycles with good times alternating the bad ones. It may be maintained that the system does not work if the trend should be broken into an economic stagnation interrupted by very short and weak revivals. The answer is that no financial system, and no political system, will long sustain such a development. Economic stagnation calls for perhaps radical changes of the whole institutional structure of the economy, including of course its fiscal system, but this reform cannot be carried out simply by fiscal policy.[54]

In this presentation the modest capital allotted to the 'budget equalization fund' was in fact allowing for limitless deficits during bad years: as an historian I may be permitted to wonder if Myrdal was less than candid in presenting the virtues of the Swedish reform to the American audience, or was the definition of business cycles the crux of the matter? When he wrote this article in 1938 the Swedish government was already applying a clearly restrictive fiscal policy in spite of an unemployment level of 8 per cent. Perhaps the temptation of presenting Sweden as a virtuous example was too strong to resist.

At this point some of Myrdal's arguments still need clarification. As he himself acknowledges, the counter-cyclical policy assumes 'business cycles with good times alternating bad ones' but how are they properly to be defined? The question of differentiating between different kinds investments was also only at an initial stage.

Still there are several points of theoretical interest to retain from these early attempts by Myrdal to develop the principles for a coherent financial and economic policy meant to counter the economic depression in the 1930's.

First: in any discussion about public accounting systems one must go beyond accepting presented balances as 'facts'. Figures in accounting systems depend on theoretical assumptions. Notably assumptions on what should be considered to be investments or not, what should be viewed as productive and profitable or not. Furthermore – even at that time there were large latitudes in concealing debts and assets, as well as making them appear in accounting places suitable for the argument that was developed. Myrdal's general reservation on the question of public finance is even more important today.

Institutions and attitudes matter. This fundamental message was later developed by Myrdal as a social scientist, but it is also present in this discussion. What might appear as a technical discussion on public accounting was in essence a question of institutions and attitudes. Established prejudices such as fear of debts and deficits was inducing an irrational and counterproductive fiscal policy. It was by advocating a new understanding of the concept of 'soundness' in public finance, and of the positive effects of deficit spending, that attitudes could be changed.

Myrdal widened the question far beyond immediately marketable assets by referring the question of 'soundness' to the totality of assets and liabilities in the public sector. By observing that the degree of soundness to be kept up was a principle that could only be established by a political decision he made political valuations the ultimate arbiter also on accounting issues. This level-headed discussion on the soundness of public finances needs to be retained when we are analysing the questions of public debts and deficits in EU countries, a problem discussed in recent years. The 'gross debt ratio' presently used to define problems of public finance obviously fails to establish a rational discussion on soundness, since it omits not only financial assets but also tangible assets in public infrastructure, broadly defined.

On the question of budget deficits Myrdal's argument that they should be made '*ostentatiously visible*' also merits some attention. He still held to the view that running costs should be balanced over a business cycle. This was the task allotted to the five-year amortization scheme. But attempts to conceal existing deficits were counterproductive. The only way to counter irrational and ideologically biased aversions against deficits was transparency, and to openly explain the necessity and positive effects of public deficits in times of crisis. This approach – openly to counter existing biased opinions – seems commendable, but is too seldom used.

At the outbreak of the financial and economic crisis in the autumn of 2008 it seemed at first that lessons had been learned. The governments of the major OECD countries were pursuing massive deficit spending policies: bailing out some banks on the verge of collapse, providing guarantees for other banks and large industries in need of liquidities (especially companies related to the car industry) and promising joint efforts to stabilize the global financial system. In the wake of the rapid slowdown of the economies that nevertheless took place in 2009 fiscal deficits soared even more, as a direct consequence of lowered fiscal revenues, due to drastically increased unemployment.

But in the second wave of the crisis, basically as a direct consequence of these measures to mitigate the financial crisis, the questions of the vulnerability of public finances in some of the EU countries came to the fore. And in that wave the major financial institutions (The IMF, BCE), the EU Commission and the various European governments seemed to have forgotten such lessons entirely, advocating austerity measures against the symptoms (the public deficits) instead of addressing the disease proper, the flaws of the prevailing economic and financial system.

It would seem unimaginable that responsible economists could have forgotten the negative effects on the economy as a whole of cutting down public expenses and raising taxes. And that in a situation of massive unemployment and zero economic growth: a situation where the public sector economy is vastly more important than it was when Myrdal first made his point.

Myrdal's earlier argument on the cumulative causations in creating vicious circles clearly comes to mind.

Out of the war: planning for peace and welfare society

Myrdal devoted the years that followed his contribution to the Swedish discussion on budget matters, to important and extensive research on social relations in the US, more specifically in a Carnegie Foundation funded project on '*The Negro Problem*'. From 1938 he was far away from the inertia of Swedish politics, but the problems of public finance never left him altogether. In 1942, when he could finally see the completion of his enormous research project on the 'American Dilemma', he declared in a letter to a friend in *Rockefeller Foundation*:

> Upon coming home I would ordinarily, as previously, have taken on – beside my professional duties – responsibilities for research and economic planning under the Swedish Government which for me, would have implied not only additional income but, particularly, research facilities which I am not provided with at the University Institute. This time, when I, because of my long absence from Sweden, have already interrupted such entanglements, I want to utilize this opportunity to keep free for work on problems of international scope. My plans are thus, not to take on any new duties in Sweden except my professorship at the University of Stockholm, but to devote the next couple of years entirely to my old interest in public finance.[55]

This wish to stay aloof from Swedish politics was quite understandable: not only had the efforts of Gunnar and Alva Myrdal to reformulate economic and social policies of the thirties been largely rebuffed by the Social Democracy to which they belonged. Still more painful was their experience in 1940. When they daringly returned to Sweden in the midst of the German onslaught on Scandinavia to share the hardships and challenges of their fellow countrymen in what Myrdal called their 'patriotic duty' they found that their party leadership regarded them more as an embarrassment than as an asset.[56]

Before any grants on Myrdal's desired project on public finance were forthcoming, he would however together with Alva Myrdal be dragged into a very intense period of planning the Swedish economic and social policy for the post-war years. Together with her friends in the Women's movement of Social Democracy Alva Myrdal, was one of the instigators of a call to the confederation of Swedish trade unions, *Landsorganisationen*, to set up a 'Labour Movement Peace Planning Council', *Arbetarrörelsens Fredsråd*. When this was set up in 1943 she was one of its members and Gunnar Myrdal was attached as an expert on economic affairs. Formally it was set up by the trade union movement, but the fact that Ernst Wigforss was the council's chairman gave the council its semi-official character. Wigforss was at the time Minister of Finance and member of the Social Democratic Party's inner circle.

The internal discussions of this council showed how far the Myrdal's had developed their views on the future role of public sector in economy.[57] Originally the prospects proposed by the Minister of Finance were, that a period of deflation, and of falling price levels were to be expected after the war. This was welcomed in general by the trade union movement and the Social Democratic party, since it would enable real wages to rise – if only the war time wages control were prolonged. The central problem of economic policy was presented as how to maintain a proper rate of deflation without causing unemployment.

The contributions of the Alva and Gunnar Myrdal – carried forward by their war time experiences of the debates in Britain and the United States – were to alter this focus drastically. The economic policies should have objectives going much further than to even out the variations of the business cycles. The aim should explicitly be to plan for full employment. 'A machine at full steam' was one of the leading themes of the programme that eventually came out of these discussions.

The role of the state should henceforward be to safeguard full employment of the work force as well as of other production factors. In view of the vast amount of internal needs that had been held back during the war, but above all in view of the vast reconstruction efforts needed in the war-torn countries, Sweden had to pursue a persistently expansive economic policy. It was with reference to the US experience of war-time economic expansion that Gunnar Myrdal claimed the possibility of such a policy, with the Swedish state in the role of planner and organizer.

Alva Myrdal's contribution was influenced by the debates in Great Britain. She was impressed by William Beveridge's social welfare plans[58] and the idea voiced in the British Labour Party of attaining 'socialism from the consumption side', she presented a new rationale for the social reforms demanded by the labour movement: pensions, child benefits, access to housing, expansion of education and health services.[59]

Characteristically Gunnar Myrdal supported this argument by saying that the main danger as he saw it as an economist, was that the efforts devoted to social reform might be viewed too narrowly, with the eyes of traditional prudence in budgetary matters. Given the rapid economic growth of the production sector, and induced by the general economic policy, social reforms must be viewed on a grand scale to balance the rapid growth in production that could be expected as a result of an economy operating 'at full steam'. The idea implicit in this argument is that social reforms are not a luxury, a cost, that the population can afford only when resources are available. Social reforms are instead a necessary part of a balanced economic development. Although Myrdal didn't use the term, we might today talk about it as a necessary balance between production and reproduction. Reproduction is not simply something that you can 'afford' – it is a vital prerequisite for production in any modern society. The conclusions of these discussions were presented in May 1944 as 'Arbetarrörelsens Efterkrigsprogram' (Post-war Program of the Labour Movement). It was a programme that not only served as electoral manifesto for the parliamentary elections in the autumn of 1944 but as a venerated reference for the labour movement during the following post-war years.

By the time this programme was published Myrdal had already shifted his focus. In 1943 he had been designated as the government's special envoy to make 'an investigation concerning Sweden's future trade relations with transocean countries'. To that effect he had spent three months in the autumn of 1943 in the US, enquiring into the state of affairs and on ongoing discussions concerning post-war planning in the US. It s is hardly surprising that Myrdal had returned to favour in government circles in Sweden at that time. As an outspoken pro-American, he was well suited to allay the suspicions in US political and business circles against Sweden, that had been neutral or – as some in the Allied countries claimed – passively pro-German during the war. The result of this mission was twofold, the publication of Myrdal's own 'post-war Manifesto', *Varning för fredsoptimism* (Warning for Post-War Optimism)[60] and his nomination as Chairman of the Swedish Post-war Economic Planning Commission.

Both the publication of this book and his chairmanship had the same overriding concern, that of convincing public opinion in general, and economic and the economic and political elites especially, of the way forward for Sweden after the Second World War.

In the internal discussions in the 'Peace Council' of the labour movement Myrdal had advocated a much more ambitious objective for economic policies than counterbalancing the business cycles: that is full employment and 'a machine at full steam'. In *Varning för fredsoptimism*, he used the American experience of wartime economy as proof for the viability of such an ambition:

'The armament efforts accomplished what the New Deal never managed to do: to put the enormous productive capacities of the American economy in full use.' He advanced three reasons for this:

1. The armament means an expansion of purchase power of a completely different scale than that of the New Deal – more than tenfold. 2. The armament is carried out by a centrally planned economy with means of compulsion. 3. The armament and the means to achieve it are accepted by the business leaders as a necessary and wise national policy, which was never the case with the New Deal in spite of its modest measures.[61]

Myrdal proceeded with an analysis of the latest developments of the US economy, showing that this rapid industrial expansion had been of mutual benefit to workers and businesses: real wages had grown and so had industrial profits.

In Myrdal's opinion this showed that an economic policy focused on economic growth could unite the concerns of modern industrialists and workers, if only the dimension of government intervention was appropriate. That is: at the level of the US wartime experience.

But if that was the case, the question was how to convince a Swedish business opinion generally reticent towards public expenditures? On this account Myrdal was guided by his acute awareness of the role of anticipations.

Varning för fredsoptimism has generally been accused of being overly pessimistic. If so, there was a reason behind it: influencing the expectations of the public was part of making it possible to supersede the dilemma posed by public war indebtedness.

It is true that he painted the depression fears in the US in very stark colours. What was feared among most US economists at the time was a replay of the thirties' depression after the war. They had in mind both the depression after the First World War, and above all they thought of the long depression period in the thirties. This fear was very much alive in American public opinion as well as among economists. Whether these fears – and Myrdal's account of them – was overly pessimistic or not is debatable: one might just as well argue that this heightened awareness among US economists about the danger of US receding in depression was one of the factors that enabled this development to be avoided. Hindsight always offers easy prognoses.

This critique however, misses the central purpose of Myrdal's post-war manifesto: to develop a post-war national project that could be 'accepted by the business leaders as a necessary and wise national policy'. To accomplish this Myrdal had to paint the dangers as well as the promises in stark colours.

This was also the purpose of the extensive engagement of Sweden in the international economic reconstruction prepared by Swedish authorities in 1944–1945. By decisions of the Swedish parliament vast resources were put at the disposal of the central bank, enabling the government to grant long term credit and trade agreements with all war-torn countries. This was a way not only of restoring the image of Sweden, tarnished by its wartime economic collaboration with Nazi Germany, but also a way of securing the interests of Swedish export industries in the uncertain times ahead.[62]

One of the paramount problems discussed among economists in Sweden during the war had been the rapid growth of public indebtedness, with budget deficits of more than 25 per cent in excess of revenues between 1940 and 1943.[63] It had been argued that soundness of public finances demanded, that the end of the war should be followed by several years of restrictive financial policies, in order to reduce public indebtedness to pre-war levels. This would evidently have jeopardized the aspirations of the labour movement for social reforms and better living conditions. The problem was discussed in the 'Peace Council', and in a Memorandum Myrdal provided a typical answer. The dilemma between repaying debt as a moral obligation, and the urge for social reforms, was transcended by reframing the problem. The problem was not the amount of public debt but its relative weight:

> Suppose that a further increase of the indebtedness is needed for some expenditures concerning schools, social policy or fighting unemployment, and assuming, which is quite reasonable, that these expenditures are increasing the national income to the extent that the revenues of government added by this increase in general revenues are greater

than the incurred costs of interest and amortization of the increased public debt. In such a case the increase in public indebtedness is well founded even from a strictly public financial point of view, regardless of the previous level of indebtedness. In other words, the increase in public indebtedness makes it easier to handle the even previously large public debt.[64]

Thus by placing the problem in a larger frame, and by taking the growth effects into account, there was no contradiction between the concerns of financial soundness and the demands for social reforms. Reforms financed by an expansionist economic policy. This was an argument directed as much towards business interests as to excessively prudent Social Democrats.

In 1944 Myrdal tried to have this view accepted as a new norm for financial policy.[65] In a discussion within the Post-war Planning Commission the future principle of public finance was discussed. It was a high-level discussion where the heads of the Swedish Central Bank, the employer's organization and the liberal party were present. In this discussion Myrdal declared that he was sceptical towards 'the wish to stabilize the public indebtedness at its present level' and 'the old worn out notion about deficit financing only for productive purposes'. Since these principles had not been applied during the war years he considered them to be ripe for change. Looking 'quite rationally on the problem of public debt' he proposed a principle exactly along the lines he had advanced one year earlier in the internal discussion with Ernst Wigforss in the 'Peace Council'.

It was primarily Dag Hammarskjöld who formulated the counter-argument. The fact that financial policy during the war had been of an unprincipled character didn't mean that one shouldn't return to the principles established in 1938: 'The budget fund should thus vary around a point of equilibrium that was the budgetary expression of the objective of keeping the volume of public wealth constant'. The norm proposed by Myrdal lacked that neutrality:

> The norm has an étatist element. It does not necessarily mean an ongoing socialization. That depends on how the state is organizing the different elements. But the norm will undoubtedly create a larger mortgage of the state in the national wealth and the national income.

With the opposition from Dag Hammarskjöld, who was not only chairman of the central bank but also the deputy of Wigforss in the Ministry of Finance, it was evident that Myrdal's foray into defining new principles for financial policy was stopped, even if it later on became commonplace in welfare state economics. This discussion, carefully transcribed by Myrdal's personal secretary Tore Browaldh, is interesting also from a methodological point of view. Where Hammarskjöld is preoccupied with norms that should secure the perfect 'neutrality' of the state in financial politics Myrdal exhibits a quite pragmatic attitude to these norms: 'they are not scientific truths, merely rules of conduct that we establish in advance.'[66]

The Planning Commission Myrdal chaired had a very broad representation. It included not only all opposition party leaders (with exception of the communists), but also the major leaders of the Employer's Association and of the banks, the trade unions, the farmers and the cooperative movement. As chairman of the Planning Commission, Myrdal was convinced of the possibility of working out a common and comprehensive post-war economic plan. In this discussion 'rational' and 'modern' were adjectives often used – based on a compromise, or rather common interest, between labour and industrialists. The different aspects of that project were developed by Myrdal both in the public debate and inside the Commission in its multiple reports.

On fiscal policy he acknowledged the misgivings of industrialists about the high levels of taxation, while at the same time turning it the other way around in an article on the profile of future tax policies. In an essay written in the autumn of 1944 – 'Höga skatter och låga räntor' (High Taxes and Low Interest Rates) – he outlined the principles of the post-war fiscal policy. Of course taxation had to be kept at a high level, he argued, due to pent up demands on government intervention. But this should not be an obstacle for modern industrialists, as the taxation on capital would only concern dividends, deductions should be allowed for all items of investments. Furthermore the government was bent on keeping the interest rates at a low level, thus favouring industrial expansion.[67]

In the Planning Commission great effort was devoted to the questions of industrial policy, geared towards favouring the concerns of 'modern industrialists'. One of the problems singled out by an investigation on the structure of different sectors of Swedish economy was the very uneven development within each line of trade, where laggard sectors would be impediments for the development of trade as a whole. To further modernization in Swedish industries and agriculture, the report of the Commission's experts advocated that measures of 'structural rationalization' sectorwise be undertaken.[68] More important still was the report produced by the experts of the Commission on 'Investment Adjustments'. Here the basis of a new design for countercyclical economic policy was developed. The premise was the inefficiency of using expenditures in public works as a demand regulator: time lags often made these measures come into effect too late and sometimes inopportunely. In this report the investment level was singled out as the dynamic element that had to be adjusted. By closely following investment planning in different sectors of the economy, early signs of changes in business cycles could be detected and acted upon. This could also have the merit – in the liberal minded view – of reducing the necessary dimension of public expenditures: 'It is wiser to stem in the brook than in the river' was the argument given. The report suggested that an investment council should be established, jointly representing business interests and the government, in order to coordinate investment policies with conjuncture policies.[69]

These endeavours to formulate a basis for a new post-war industrial and economic policy are still of considerable theoretical interest. The relevance of Myrdal's argument on the necessarily political, value-laden content of economic theories was however clearly vindicated by the reception of these ideas, and of the reports of the Swedish Post-war Planning commission in general. None of these suggestions on industrial policy were accepted by the business representatives in the Commission.

The post-war years were in fact characterized by intense ideological struggles in Sweden between the new Social Democratic government and the Liberal and Conservative opposition parties, supported by the resources of the Swedish confederation of employers, SAF.

In what was termed *Planhushållningsdebatten* (the debate on economic planning) these parties were arguing that the government pursued a policy aimed at establishing a planned economy, in short socialism. In fact, the reform agenda of the government was quite modest, mainly keeping the war time taxation level in place in order to finance some social reforms (increasing state pensions, introducing child benefits and expanding the education system and social housing schemes). In these ideological debates Myrdal played a prominent role, since he had been chairing the economic post-war planning and had become Minister of Commerce in the post-war Social Democratic government formed in August 1945. As Minister of Commerce it was his task to work out the international trade agreements needed, and also to enact the proposals on industrial policy developed by the planning commission.

Myrdal was always eager to react to ideological challenges. In a speech to the industrialists in Stockholm in 1946 he characteristically accepted the liberal accusation of *planhushållning* (planned economy) in a paradoxical way so as to wrench it out of opposition hands. He argued that the tendency towards increased planning of the economy was not something pursued by any special political party, but a secular trend coming out of the centralizing tendencies in the privately owned business world, and out of the increased demands on government intervention resulting from the wars and the economic crises: 'The demand on a planned economy has in practice arisen out of a need to coordinate already present and unavoidable state interventions in a rational and just way.' He even argued that this was evidenced by the ongoing discussions on international trade:

> the demand on free trade between countries is nothing else but a demand on international planning on a giant scale. To anyone who has in the least dealt with these problems theoretically or practically nothing is so annoyingly unworldly as the false notion – regrettably still current in our country – that free trade means non-intervention by the state.[70]

He described the general trend as being a development 'away from the economy of free competition', as a tendency characterized by 'centralization' and 'central direction' This was not something caused by social democracy, as their opponents claimed:

An ever so rapid glance at the establishment of the actually existing governing of markets within agriculture, industry, trade and free professions are giving a telling answer to that propaganda, as does the still continuing concentration of the financial control over credit markets and industry.

The state's responsibility for maintaining full employment was, according to Myrdal, fully acknowledged by all parties. It was also generally understood that this responsibility entailed a circumstantial state planning to stabilize a high and constant conjuncture/activity level.

In the longer run he predicted a continuing trend towards equalization of living conditions and democratization through a regulation of property rights, a development towards greater equality, transparency, democratic accountability and regulated, organized markets. Where did this leave the question of nationalization? It was a side question, Myrdal argued, the prime interest of the Social Democracy was not the socialization of the industry but it's rationalization: 'We are not interested in socialization for its own sake. Our primary interest – apart from lessened inequalities and democratization of power and responsibilities – is the rationalization of industries, not their socialization.'

And that was why he thought that there would be a common interest between this Social Democracy and the 'modern industrialists'. He obviously saw this process of increased planning and rationality as secular, rooted in the irreversible acceptance of the universal suffrage and the logic of full employment. It is difficult to know to what extent this conviction at that moment was a genuine one, or if it was one dictated by his overall aim as a politician: to inspire confidence among the business community that the long term economic policy proposed by the government was rational and mutually advantageous. In other words to have this policy 'accepted by the business leaders as a necessary and wise national policy', as was the case with the US wartime policies.

The subsequent events in 1946–1947 would however show that neither the industrialists nor the liberal and conservative opinion makers would accept this increased weight of the state, this fading away of their power privileges, as gracefully as Myrdal had hoped. Under the banner of 'resistance against the planned economy' and against what was termed as the social democratic 'misgovernment' the political opposition and its affiliated press raised a campaign ultimately aimed at the elections in 1948. Only their failure to defeat the Social Democratic government paved the way for subsequent compromises between Social Democracy and the leaders of the Swedish industry.

Well before that a politically motivated conflict over a Swedish–Soviet Trade Agreement in late 1946 made Myrdal the scapegoat of the liberal and conservative press. Moreover when he found himself marginalized within the government, notably the Minister of Finance, and thus unable to influence it on measures to be taken prior to a currency crisis, Myrdal felt disappointed. In March 1947 he eagerly seized the opportunity to leave Swedish politics for an international career as Executive Secretary of the UN Economic Commission for Europe, the UNECE.

Instead of devoting himself to studies in 'public finance' as he had wished in 1942, Gunnar Myrdal had been in the centre of Swedish politics and political debates during the five ensuing years. Evidently this did not leave room for him to write comprehensively on financial theory and policy, but, as we have seen, in the course of these actions he opened new areas for theoretical reflection. Even if Myrdal's attempts to develop a post-war national project for Sweden were thwarted there are several lines of thought worth retaining from this endeavour.

- Myrdal was a pioneer in insisting on the proactive role of the government on economic issues. Since anticipation played a vital role in the dynamics of the economy it was essential that the government could provide comprehensive and broadly based long-term planning, guiding the anticipations towards an overall ambition for the long term development.
- The overall ambition assigned was higher than before the war, it was geared towards maintaining full employment of labour as well as of other productive forces. It was thus an ostentatiously pro-growth orientation, growth being understood as growth of the aggregate

economy and not only of production. This growth orientation partly provided a solution to the dilemma of increased indebtedness caused by the war: it was not by austerity measures that the debt towards creditors should be repaid but in the longer run by the resources created through economic growth.

• An interesting feature of the economic policy proposed was that it was intended as investment management, not the demand management as was usually the case with 'Keynesian' economics. That is: it favoured growth-oriented investment policies.

• The insistence on maintaining the high taxation levels of the war signalled an orientation towards balanced growth: it was argued by Myrdal that education might properly be understood as investment rather than running costs in public finance. This argument could easily be expanded towards understanding not only educational costs but also social reforms and health costs, not as a luxury to be offered once the economy permitted it, but as the necessary reproduction component of the social growth of society.

• Finally the international component should be signalled. The large frame of the Swedish measures can be seen as an attempt at a 'Marshall Plan' before the hour. The political content of which was yet another attempt at transcending dilemmas: after the horrendous human losses and destruction caused by the war it was a contribution aiming at reconciliation through complimentary growth.

In the aftermath of 2008 we are now in a radically different situation. But Myrdal's approach to post-war economic policies nevertheless seems to be in need of further exploration in just as many areas. Many of those who proclaimed the victory of market economy at the end of the Cold War now seem to be in disarray after the several financial crises. Many are now re-affirming the role of the state – and of international institutions fulfilling a similar function. However in a situation where indebtedness is becoming a pervasive phenomenon nationally and internationally: what should that role be, how should one deal with debt? Can Myrdal's discussion of the debt problem and of how to transcend the dilemma between financial 'soundness' and welfare after the war also be relevant today?

Can there be a complementary way out of tensions, a new 'Marshall Plan' in view of increased international tensions in an economic climate characterized by unequal growth patterns and dark horizons? Or more to the point an International, a World New Deal such as that called for by US liberals like Lewis Lorwin? This latter question brings us to the area of international economy and the development of Myrdal's theories in that area, to which we will now turn.

Notes

1 A more comprehensive overview of the life and works of Gunnar Myrdal is presented in the above-mentioned *The Essential Gunnar Myrdal* (2005).
2 A fascinating and searching account of this relationship is given by the Swedish historian Yvonne Hirdman in *Alva Myrdal: The Passionate Mind* (Bloomington, IN: Indiana University Press, 2008).
3 The information on Alva's advice given by Gunnar Myrdal to Stellan Andersson, the organizer of *Alva and Gunnar Myrdal's Archives* at the *Archives and Library of the Labour Movement* in Stockholm, Sweden.
4 First presented in B. Ohlin, *Interregional and International Trade* (Cambridge, MA: Harvard University Press, 1932). Succinctly put, the theorem states that international trade is due to the fact that countries have different relative scarcities of factors of production giving each country specific comparative advantages. Trade would tend to equalize prices by lowering prices on scarce factors of production and raising prices on factors of production that are in abundance.
5 The Swedish term of the discipline – 'Nationalekonomi' – denotes the discipline's relation to a political subject – the nation. Its proper equivalent in English is thus rather the traditional denomination of 'Political Economy' than the currently conventional term 'Economics'.
6 Gustav Cassel, *Theory of Social Economy* (London: Fisher Unwin, 1923).
7 Cassel (1923), p. vii.
8 G. Myrdal, *Prisbildningsproblemet och föränderligheten* (Price Formation and the Change Factor) (Stockholm: Almqvist & Wicksell, 1927).
9 Myrdal, *Prisbildningsproblemet* (1927), p. 8. Also in *The Essential Gunnar Myrdal* (2005), p. 30.
10 G. Myrdal, *Vetenskap och politik i nationalekonomien* (Stockholm: Norstedts, 1930) (Science and politics in the Political Economy), later in English as G. Myrdal, *The Political Element in the Development of Economic Theory* (London: Routledge & Kegan Paul, 1953) and several later editions.
11 Myrdal, *Vetenskap och politik i nationalekonomien* (1930), pp. 11–12. (Translation ÖA).
12 G. Myrdal: 'Den förändrade världsbilden inom nationalekonomien' (The Altered World View in Political Economy) in *Krisen och samhällsvetenskaperna. Två installationsföreläsningar* (Stockholm: Kooperativa Förbundet, 1935). Quotations in pp. 8–12 (Translation ÖA).
13 From Myrdal's preface to the 1972 edition of *Vetenskap och politik I nationalekonomien.*
14 Simply presented by Myrdal, beliefs pretend knowledge, valuations pertains to what is 'just', 'right', 'fair' or 'desirable' – or the opposite: 'One of these types of conception is intellectual and cognitive; the other is emotional and volitive.' G. Myrdal, *Objectivity in Social Research. The Wimmer Lectures* (New York: Pantheon Books, 1969), p. 15.
15 As Giovanni Arrighi has shown in *Adam Smith in Beijing: Lineages of the Twentyfirst Century* (London: Verso, 2007) this metaphor unjustly attributed to Adam Smith should rather be ascribed to nineteenth -century economists such as Leon Walras and Alfred Marshall.
16 G. Myrdal, 'Institutional economics' *Journal of Economic Issues*, Vol. XII, No. 4 (1978), pp. 773–783.

17 The Association of Evolutionary Economists (www.afee.net)and The Institute for New Economic Thinking (www.inet.org)are two important sources of research.
18 http://ineteconomics.org/blog/inet/edward-fullbrook-toxic-textbooks.
19 Myrdal, *Prisbildningsproblemet* (1927), p. 5.
20 Ibid.
21 Ibid., p. 8. Also in *The Essential Gunnar Myrdal* (2005), p. 31.
22 Myrdal, *Prisbildningsproblemet* (1927), p. 12 (Translation ÖA).
23 Ibid., p. 14.
24 A presentation of Wicksell's ideas is found in Gilles Dostaler: 'Les grands auteurs de la pensée économique' (*Alternatives économiques, Hors-série Poche* no 57, Novembre 2012), pp. 138–141.
25 G. Myrdal: 'Om penningteoretisk jämvikt: en studie over den "normala räntan" I Wicksells penninglära' [*On Monetary Equilibrium: A Study on the 'Normal Rate of Interest' in the monetary doctrine of Knut Wicksell*] published in *Ekonomisk Tidskrift* in1931. Later developed and published as *Monetary Equilibrium* (London: William Hodge & Co, 1939).
26 Myrdal, *Prisbildningsproblemet* (1927), p. 255.
27 Ibid., p. 20. Also in *The Essential Gunnar Myrdal* (2005), p. 31.
28 G. Myrdal, *Monetary Equilibrium* (London: W. Hodge & Co Ltd, 1939), p. 47.
29 Ibid.
30 Ibid., p. 32.
31 Notably in J. Stiglitz, *Globalization and its Discontents* (London: Allen Lane/ Penguin Books, 2002).
32 The idea of a 'Third World' was frequent during the Cold War era, as a designation of the non-aligned countries that wanted to stay out of the two blocs formed by the Western industrial countries and Japan (the First World) and the Soviet Union and its allies in state-planned economies (the Second World).
33 Robert Skidelsky, *Keynes: The return of the Master* (London: Allen Lane, 2009). A Gaussian curve means a clock-like representation around a centre .
34 Nassim Nicholas Taleb, *The Black Swan: The Impact of the Highly Improbable* (London: Allen Lane, 2007).
35 Myrdal, *Om penningteoretisk jämvikt* (1931), p. 255.
36 Ibid., p. 195.
37 This was the common assumption of economists, basing themselves on the so-called Say's law.
38 Myrdal (1939), p. 184. Also in W. J. Barber (2008), p. 29.
39 Statistics in the BIS Triennal Report 1998, quoted from P. Hirst and G. Thompson, *Globalization in Question* (Cambridge: Polity Press, 1999), p. 50.
40 *BIS Quarterly Review*, September 2008, Tables 19 and 23. Worth noting is that 85 per cent of this trading took place outside organized exchanges, that is, over-the-counter (OTC).
41 For instance, Hyman Minsky, *Stabilizing an Unstable Economy* (New Haven, CT: Yale University Press, 1986).
42 G. Myrdal, *Sveriges väg genom penningkrisen* (Stockholm: Natur och Kultur, 1931).
43 Published also as G. Myrdal, *Konjunktur och offentlig hushållning. En utredning* (Stockholm: Kooperativa föbundets bokförlag, 1933). The title can be roughly translated as ('Business Cycle and Public Economy: An Investigation) (Translation ÖA).
44 Myrdal (1933), p. 5.

45 Ibid., p. 19.
46 Ibid., p. 20.
47 Ibid., p. 25.
48 A more detailed treatment of the policies of the time is given in Örjan Appelqvist: 'Keynes et le socialisme démocratique en Suède', in D. Cohen and A. Bergougounioux (eds), *Le socialism à l'épreuve du capitalisme* (Paris: Fayard, 2012).
49 On the complex relationship between Gunnar Myrdal and Dag Hammarskjöld, see Örjan Appelqvist, 'A Hidden Duel: Gunnar Myrdal and Dag Hammarskjöld in Economics and International Politics 1935–1955', *Stockholm Papers in Economic History*, No 2. (2008); 'A Hidden Duel: Gunnar Myrdal and Dag Hammarskjöld in Economics and International Politics 1935–1955' *Stockholm Working Papers on Economic History (SWoPEc)*, No 2). Available online.
50 In a situation where the automatic annual swings amounted to 200–250 million Swedish krona in the years between 1920 and 1937, the budget equalizations fund was allotted a meagre 37 million krona in 1938.
51 G. Myrdal, 'Fiscal Policy in the Business Cycle', *American Economic Review*, 1939. Quotes from *The Essential Gunnar Myrdal* (2005), pp. 35–46.
52 Ibid., p. 38.
53 Ibid., p. 45.
54 Ibid., p. 46.
55 Letter to Willits, Rockefeller Foundation, 26 May 1942. *Personal archives of Alva and Gunnar Myrdal*, 08. vol 016. Emphasis in the original.
56 Described in more detail in Appelqvist, *Bruten Brygga. Gunnar Myrdal och Sveriges ekonomiska efterkrigspolitik 1943–1947* (Stockholm: Santérus, 2000), pp. 58–60.
57 The minutes of these deliberations are kept in the archives of the council, at *Labour Movement Archives and Library (ARAB)*, Stockholm.
58 William Beveridge (1879–1963) was a liberal economist and social reformer. His Report *Social Insurances and Allied Services* published in 1942 provided the main line of British post-war social reforms.
59 The proposals of William Beveridge and the Labour Party discussions on social reforms were presented to the Swedish audience by Alva Myrdal in *Stickprov från Storbritannien* (Stockholm: Bonniers, 1942).
60 G. Myrdal, *Varning för Fredsoptimism [Warning against Post-War Optimism]* (Stockholm: Bonniers 1944). The following quotations are translated by ÖA).
61 Ibid., p. 104.
62 The frames of credit allowed to the Central Bank in 1944–1945 amounted to 2.5 million krona, more than half of the yearly budget at that time.
63 Accounts specified in Appelqvist (2000), Appendix 4.
64 Memorandum by Gunnar Myrdal dated June 1943. Archives of the Peace Council, Vol. 3:3, *ARAB*, Stockholm. Quoted in Appelqvist (2000), p. 80.
65 Transcript from meeting 29 June 1944. *Archives of Alva and Gunnar Myrdal* (AGM),06.1.019. Participants in the meeting were Gunnar Myrdal as chairman of the Commission, Gustaf Söderlund, deputy chairman of the Commission and Head of the Swedish Employers Association, Dag Hammarskjöld, chairman of the Swedish Central Bank and the party leader of the Liberals Bertil Ohlin. Appelqvist (2000), p. 228.
66 Quotations from transcript above.

67 This profile, which characterizes Sweden's fiscal policy in the post-war years rather well, was first presented as a contribution in a book dedicated to the economist Eli Heckscher. Gunnar Myrdal: 'Höga skatter och låga räntor', *Studier i Ekonomi och Historia.Tillägnade Eli f. Heckscher* (Stockholm: Bonniers, 1944).

68 'Promemoria XII:1 angående industrins strukturella rationalisering', Archives of *Kommissionen för ekonomisk efterkrigsplanering (Keep), vol 19*, in *Riksarkivet* (Sweden National Archives).

69 Report concerning investment adjustments published as Commission Report in *Statens Offentliga Utredningar (SOU)* 57 (1944), pp. 85–87.

70 Quotes here and following from Gunnar Myrdal: 'Staten och industrin' (The state and the industry). Speech, 8 January 1946 to Stockholm's Köpmannaklubb (Association of Stockholm Merchants), published in *Industria*, 42, 1946, pp. 41–50.

2 Gunnar Myrdal and the international economy

Gunnar Myrdal's research interest was from the outset very much conditioned by Swedish concerns, be it on matters of response to the economic crisis in 1931 or concerning social policy on demographic issues. He was however at the same time from the very outset heavily influenced by international discussions. The discussions in the United States were particularly important and formative for him.

In 1929–1930, at the height of the unravelling economic crisis he and Alva Myrdal were Rockefeller research fellows in New York, where they could see the human tragedies caused by the crisis firsthand. Between 1938 and 1942 he was directing a major social research project on 'the Negro Question', which was to lead to the publication of *An American Dilemma* in 1944. During this period he was deeply immersed in American discussions not only on social issues but also on general economic issues. But it was not until he was back in Sweden in late 1942 that he started to engage himself actively in discussions on the future of international economic relations.

Forging the international outlook during the war: bridge-building and 'organized free trade'

Alva Myrdal played an important role by convincing Gunnar that he should address questions on international politics and economics during the war years. She established herself as columnist on international affairs in various Social Democratic newspapers in Sweden and her speciality was post-war planning discussions in the United Kingdom, a subject about which she had considerable expertise.[1]

The network of Social Democratic refugees living in Stockholm during the war provided another source of inspiration on international affairs for Myrdal. In the autumn of 1942 some prominent Norwegian-speaking Social Democrats (Martin Tranmael, Willy Brandt) presented a platform for discussion on which peace objectives to promote once victory over Nazi Germany was secured. Around that platform a group of some 35 members from the major European countries was constituted, *Internationale Gruppe Demokratischen Sozialisten (IGDS)*.[2] Gunnar and Alva Myrdal joined the group from the start and it was the beginning of life-long friendships with among others Willy Brandt and Bruno Kreisky.[3] It was quite natural that Gunnar and Alva Myrdal would seek contact with Social Democratic refugees from Nazi occupied countries when trying to renew political discussions in Stockholm. When they had felt the 'patriotic duty' to return to Sweden in 1940, their offer of services had been ignored in a rather condescending manner by the Social Democratic leadership, who were at that time above all anxious not to irritate Nazi Germany. Three years later the situation had changed and there was some reason for optimism among anti-Nazi intellectuals. The IGDS group published a manifesto in May 1943 in the monthly magazine of the Swedish Trade Union Confederation, *Fackföreningsvärlden*. The manifesto advocated a peace settlement that would not be a repetition of the catastrophic Versailles Treaty, but built on democratic renewal and efforts at building bridges between Western and Eastern parts of Europe – the Soviet Union included. Once Nazi Germany was defeated, the challenge would be to begin the economic reconstruction on an all-European basis, where neutral countries run by Social Democratic parties might hopefully play a constructive role.

Many of these ideas were elaborated further by Myrdal in the above mentioned book on the post-war challenges, his *Varning för fredsoptimism*. In the previous chapter his attempts to gain domestic support for his post-war economic planning project were highlighted. This work is of such vital importance in understanding Myrdal's international outlook in general, that it is necessary to expand the presentation of the themes developed in the book.

Varning för fredsoptimism – so far only translated into German – is an excellent piece of political and economic analysis written at a moment when the terms of the future peace settlement were still very open.[4] It is typical of Myrdal's approach: pessimistic scenarios are vividly described, alternated with appeals to belief in the force of ideas and a firm optimism when it comes to meeting challenges. What was needed according to him was 'people that managed to be dreamers as well as realists, people with burning hearts and cool, well-trimmed brains.'[5]

Varning för fredsoptimism describes the actual state of the negotiations between the US and the UK concerning the principles of the post-war international trade and the discussions in the League of Nations office at Princeton, N.Y. on the same questions. It also contains an analysis of the errors made by the Versailles Treaty in 1919 after the First World War, and a discussion about the actual tendencies in American politics at the turning point of the war.

As the title indicates (Beware of Peace Optimism) he is above all focused on warning the Swedish public against lightly adopted optimism. In the Foreword he states that, 'The aim of the book is above all to shatter illusions'.[6]

His warnings concern the situation of the post-war economy just as much as international political relations after the war. He paints a broad picture of the discussion among US economists and their apprehensions about immediate post-war development.

One of the illusions that Myrdal wanted to shatter was the belief that the war time conditions of the market would be stabilized in the post-war period: 'America is probably entering a very unruly economic development after the war. It is even probable that the American economy rather shortly after the war will relapse into a deep depression and mass unemployment.'[7] At the time it was a rather commonplace apprehension among US economists, which later proved to be an erroneous prognosis.

The second – and major – illusion that Myrdal wanted to shatter concerned the post-war international political climate:the belief in the firm community of interests and solidarity within the United Nations Organisation and especially between the three great powers America, Great Britain and the Soviet Union.'[8] He noted that:

> the joint action against Germany is the only cooperation between the United Nations that so far has been safely established.... But the safety of this fundament is illusory, this will of course be evident quite soon, once Germany is defeated. If by then no other basis for joint action has been established it will inevitably fall apart.[9]

In Myrdal's opinion this would put Sweden in a very serious situation: 'Even if we might avoid being dragged into the war the nearest post-war years will raise very serious problems for our foreign policy, problems in the final analysis regarding our national independence.'[10]

He predicted a dire scenario:

> We will be running the risk of being confronted by currency barriers, various international or simply imperialistic controls, demands on credits and compensations. We must fear that our provision difficulties will be used as thumbscrews on us to force us to go where we don't want to go.[11]

In this apprehension he was clearly farsighted, as subsequent events would demonstrate.

Three questions were at the forefront of Myrdal's investigation: the terms of the coming post-war settlement, the conditions for re-establishing open international trade and the role Sweden might play in these areas.

Writing at the beginning of 1944, at a time when the tide of war had only recently turned, and when the impending defeat of Nazi Germany was becoming clear to convinced anti-Nazis like the Myrdals, the question he raised was a rather unexpected one: How can a vindictive peace be avoided? How to avoid a second Versailles Treaty, a settlement built on massive reparations crushing the defeated enemy – a settlement paving the way for another wave of resentments – and ensuing demands of revenge?

During the first difficult war years Gunnar and Alva Myrdal had been among the leading, principal pro-Allied propagandists.[12] They had appealed to Swedish public opinion to oppose to exaggerated timidity and opportunism in the face of German pressures. They saw the resilience of the British people and the economic and military strength of American liberalism as sources for optimism. But in *Varning för fredsoptimism* – when the Allied victory seemed clearly in sight – the problem he perceived was rather the opposite one. In the Introduction, where Myrdal presented the purpose of the book – warning against illusions – he writes: 'Almost the whole nation seems to be too happily and thoughtlessly caught by the American and British propaganda.'[13] What was needed, according to the basically pro-American Myrdal, was a 'a hard-boiled analysis' of the situation.

This analysis was clearly steeped in realistic terms. He specifically warned against any undue optimism on general psychological grounds. Even if the yearning for peace was immensely strong and shared among the populations, the war had unleashed passions that would not so easily disappear. Nationalistic animosities had been strengthened at the extreme, as a result of the occupations and the atrocities of war – and a desire for revenge were present at all levels of society in European countries that had served as a stage for war and occupation. The need for hard-boiled analysis applied also to the allied countries in the West. The fact that they were democracies in no way guaranteed that they would play a disinterested role. In Myrdal's view the 'great power imperialism' of individual countries was

> a practical necessity induced by prevailing conditions. Habits of master race are developed also in the great Western democracies. The safely acquired and well understood interests of the propertied are protected. Moral taboos are thus broken down. Codes of international justice are worn out.[14]

It was in a situation of what Myrdal characterized as '*moral fatigue*' (Idealtrötthet) that the difficult questions of peace conditions and war reparations should be settled.

Although the urge for revenge and reparations by those who had been victims of the Nazi war and occupation, were understandable, they did not represent not a solution tenable in the long run. The economic chaos produced by the harsh reparations imposed on Germany after the First World War was proof of that. Who should pay for the war? In terms of justice the answer was obvious – it was Nazi Germany that had provoked the war and devastated the countries the German army had occupied. But the results of the war presented a dilemma – a defeated and economically ruined aggressor was unable to pay for the damage it had caused.

In a twist typical of Myrdal, he claimed that there existed a way out of this dilemma. The return of a vindictive, destructive peace settlement could be avoided. The solution spelt a joint European recovery, largely financed by US financial aid. In fact: a continuation of the Lend-Lease-Agreements on a larger scale. He proposed a solution in line with the idea of a World New Deal advanced by Lewis Lorwin, and favourably judged by Myrdal in 1942.

The US war time experience had clearly shown the potential of a federally financed investment programme: with full employment of the work force the 'total value of the production' had more than doubled GDP between 1940 and 1943, real wages had grown by 45 per cent and while simultaneously corporate profits were at an all time high. The high levels of taxation – especially in the wealthier segments of the population – had provided the revenues needed to pay interest and instalments on public debt. It had in fact been a policy that increased the strength of the US not only militarily, but also economically in general.[15]

According to Myrdal the solution and the key to the post-war dilemmas in Europe clearly rested with the United States and its political and economic elites. However, in this regard Myrdal struck a pessimistic tone in *Varning för fredsoptimism* in 1944. Writing after the 1942 midterm elections he noted that it was conservative elements among Republicans and Democrats that had gained the upper hand in Congress. That shift meant breaking the alliance between the Democrats, who were close to the labour movement, and the modern industrialists in the Republican party. Roosevelt had built large parts of his economic policy on this alliance. Myrdal feared that from now on the rentier interest of bankers and conservative prudence in general would restrain the generous and audacious financial initiatives that were needed: 'the mood has changed towards an evermore suspiciously skeptical, pessimistic and nationally egoistic attitude in matters of foreign policy'.[16]

The other question raised by Myrdal – that of how to re-establish open international trade relations after the war – was connected with the origins of the war. A rather commonplace analysis was that the war was largely caused by the efforts of industrial countries to gain access to raw materials. The colonial powers had a monopolistic access to the resources of their colonies. This was an access that the emerging powers like Japan and Germany sought to wrest from the colonial powers that monopolized them (France and Great Britain) or gain by military occupation (Soviet Union). The liberal recipe as developed in the 'Atlantic Charter' in 1941 was to guarantee open access for all by a free trade regime. However Myrdal saw this as a simplistic view:

> One of the most erroneous misrepresentations in the political thought of the inter-war period – a thesis incorporated into the anti-rationalist Nazi ideology and thus not guiltless for the outbreak of the Second World War – was the thesis about scarcity of primary products. In reality one of the basic factors behind the world depression of the thirties was the overproduction of primary products. Primary products were available in abundance. They became too cheap, that was the problem. Transatlantic countries exporting primary products were impoverished. Their currencies went into disorder. To us these countries were destroyed as markets for our industrial products. There are all possibilities that the same tragic interplay will be resumed again after the Second World War at a heightened pace if not international measures are taken to raise and stabilize the prizes of primary products.[17]

The objective professed in the Atlantic Charter – free access to primary products without colonial restrictions – was consequently not a solution to the problems of international trade. 'Free access to primary products' is a relevant answer only if the question is 'scarcity' or 'scarcity at correct price levels'. This was an answer relevant only for those industries and those industrial countries that were lacking colonial access to primary products. Nor was the fluctuation of prices a major problem. While recognizing the positive aspects of the system of 'buffer stocks' proposed by Lionel Robbins it was nevertheless quite insufficient:

> The problem is in fact not only the prices are fluctuating in a harmful manner. The price levels are also generally too low pushing producer countries into poverty.... The basic faults are that the producer countries are in overpopulated, underindustrialized regions while the importing countries are striving to maintain an expensive production by protectionist measures, keeping their prices high thus restricting overall demand.[18]

It was not by extending access to colonial exploitation to non-colonial industrialized countries as well that world trade should be developed. In the thirties the lack of general demand had been one of the important factors that lead to the depression in industrialized countries. At that time Myrdal and his likeminded economists had argued the need to stimulate overall demand by an ambitious social and economic policy. When addressing the problems of developing international trade Myrdal argued much the same way: it was the lack of demand in the 'underindustrialized' countries that had to be tackled.

Any price equilibrium had, according to Myrdal, to be regarded as dependent on the institutional environment: the low prices of primary products were a result of their politically disadvantageous position in relation to consumer interests in the colonial powers. Free trade in the sense of dismantling narrowly egoistic trade barriers consequently had to be combined with an international regulation that not only stabilized fluctuations but also raised price levels generally. Such a regulation should not only further the ambition of the Atlantic Charter of lessening the needs in impoverished, exploited regions of the world, the increased overall demand in those regions would also facilitate a general international economic expansion. Referring to the objectives of the Atlantic Charter to create a 'peaceful, democratic happy new world where all people should be freed from need and fear and where the living standards of the poor and exploited regions should be raised to a level of human dignity',[19] Myrdal argued that this demanded institutional tools in the world trade far beyond establishing free competition.

In the development of these thoughts Myrdal saw himself as simply expressing the same ideas that were central to the negotiators in the current discussions on international trade:

> In the current negotiations a theory about how to handle the problem of pricing primary products is about to be developed. It will be necessary to have a cartel system. But it has to be put on a sound basis by being elevated to state-level international agreements.... In these cartel agreements importing countries should have a voting strength equal to that of producer countries when deciding upon the regulations and above all when fixing the maximal and minimal prices between which prices on primary products should be restricted.[20]

These state-level international agreements should also go beyond pricing issues:

> These agreements should incorporate measures against export subsidies as well as against customs on imports and other import barriers. In

general the purpose should be to attain an allocation of the production that is natural from an economic productivity point of view coupled with a general expansion of consumption levels. Furthermore rules should be devised to ensure that the workers in the producer countries are getting a reasonable share of the higher and stabilized prices of the primary products in terms of improved wages and working conditions.[21]

Myrdal's attitude was – as with the dilemma of the war settlement – that there was a solution to be found and a way out of colonial exploitation and impoverishment in 'underdeveloped' regions and depression in 'developed' countries, a mutually beneficial way.

After this presentation of post-war international dilemmas and their possible solutions Myrdal turned to what was the prime purpose of his book: that of characterizing Sweden's national interest in this situation, and pointing to the role Sweden might play to facilitate a solution of international dilemmas.

It must be remembered that he wrote the book as chairman of *Kommissionen för ekonomisk efterkrigsplanering*, the broadly based Commission for Economic Post-war Planning. This was a commission where leading representatives of the political parties, business interests and trade unions participated.

The rather difficult situation of Sweden towards the end of the war has already been mentioned. Sweden was quietly trying to change the bias of its neutrality, disentangling itself from the embrace of Germany, and re-establishing links with the Allies. To counter a Swedish public opinion that Myrdal regarded as 'thoughtlessly influenced by British and American propaganda', he reminded the reader that no nation had gone to war with Germany for another country's sake. Only when attacked had the countries entered into the war. Partly as a justification for Sweden's strivings to keep itself out of the war he maintained that the basic motives for the warring nations were non-ideological:

> It is true that it is the victory of the Allied powers that is saving us from being incorporated into Hitler's Nazi order. But it is not true that they are fighting for our sake. Neither great or small states have entered this war for any other reason than their own security. Most of them have been brought into the war simply because they have been attacked.[22]

And still – the post-war world had to be built on commonly shared ideals:

> the moral fatigue (idealtröttheten) is a weakness in the human basis of the actual post-war negotiations.... It does not seem improbable to me

that a future culture historian who will explain why the peace was lost after the Second World War will emphasize this moral factor. The statesmen didn't dare to take the bold steps and show the liberating generosity because they no longer had a sufficient belief in the Western ideals they had inherited.[23]

Formulating Sweden's national interest in the post-war world he wrote:

We are striving for a democratic and legally regulated supra-national order in the world. We want safety against war. We want free trade, unfettered movement of capital and a rational division of labour between nations.[24]

In essence *Varning för fredsoptimism* was an appeal to the liberal idealism of Woodrow Wilson. It was liberal also in its attitude towards solving problems in inter-state relations: stability should not be attained through politics of power balancing but by a broadening and deepening economic cooperation and by a search for consensus:

The vulnerability in our situation stems not least from the fact that we might be dragged into conflicts between the three great powers. From a Swedish point of view we must therefore ardently hope ... both that America and Great Britain will be able to establish a close and frictionless co-operation in world politics and that it will be possible to lay the foundations for a trustful co-operation between the Anglo-Saxon great powers and the Soviet Union. The latter is of vital interest for Sweden since we will otherwise easily come into the line of fire between them.[25]

The long term goal of Sweden was that the discussions on the principles of the United Nations would result in an organization based on the ideals cited above:

In such a world order we would for our part be prepared to accept essential limitations of our national sovereignty.... Such a democratic world organization is however far away: the most immediate task after the war will be to carefully pilot ourselves day by day through waters of great dangers and immense difficulties.[26]

In the immediate post-war situation Sweden should pursue what he called an 'internationalist policy of neutrality' implying 'an unreserved adherence to all reasonable strivings to reach solutions of world problems along the generally acknowledged ideals of justice, freedom, order and security but a very reserved attitude to interest motivated politics of specific great powers.'[27]

As noted above Myrdal was explicitly sceptical about any pretention of the great powers – whatever their domestic political system – to be especially benign or moral. The great divide in world politics was instead between great powers and smaller nations. In fact the smaller nations had a special responsibility for the state of world affairs. When specifying Sweden's interest in world affairs he stated:

> It is in the nature of the matter that especially a small nation – if it has reached the spiritual maturity to understand its own interest – must make its own the ideals of internationalism. We can never be tempted by political militarism or economic imperialism. Our interests are so evidently closely tied to peace, justice, international democracy and free trade.[28]

For those who wanted to leave the initiative of tracing the great patterns of world politics to the great powers he presented a paradox:

> To us as a small nation it should therefore be natural to give voice to grand politics. The great powers are on the contrary caught by their particular interests and the world around us is drenched in nationalism.[29]

The predicament of small nations was not only valid in general. In an earlier passage typical of Myrdal he even stated: 'We are by our history and our foreign relations especially chosen to be the advocates of world interest.'[30]

Throughout the book Myrdal presents an interesting blend of realism in the analysis of the motives behind national policies of different countries, and his firm belief in the power of ideas, an attitude characteristic of philosophical liberalism. Here we can clearly find a clue to his and Alva Myrdal's persistent refusal of the Cold War rhetoric in the subsequent years. Even nations with whom Sweden was friendly were primarily driven by egoistic national interests rather than the altruistic ideas they professed publicly. The major dividing line in international politics was thus not a question of ideology but of size: small nations versus the great powers.

Sweden thus chosen to be the 'advocate of world interest' – what an amazingly audacious formulation, what a surprising turnaround way he proposed to extricate Sweden from its morally difficult position in 1944 when it was cautiously loosening the German grip over its economy. And yet it was not a verbal whim but a logically coherent position grounded in a solid political and economic analysis. A joint post-war reconstruction was not only in line with the wishes of the exiled socialist politicians in the *Internationale Gruppe* in Stockholm, it was also in the interests of Swedish industrialists to facilitate the economic recovery not only in the neighbouring countries but also in the German economy. To promote trade agreements with the Soviet Union was in the same manner not only a method of entering new markets, but also of safe-guarding the independence of Finland – and thereby considerable Swedish assets in Finland.

In its general approach to economic post-war problems Myrdal's argument was very much in line with that of radical American liberals such as Lewis L. Lorwin[31] and more importantly Henry Wallace, formerly US Vice President, then acting Minister of Commerce. But there was a special twist in Myrdal's argument: it was a confluence of his radical critique of neo-classical theories in the 1930's and his interpretation of the growth possibilities shown by the US rearmament boom during the war and finally in accordance with the international discussions in IGDS on the future of Europe.

Many might find Myrdal's ambition for Sweden to be an 'advocate of world interest' overly presumptuous: indeed one of the most common criticisms levelled against Sweden's foreign policy as it was developed after the Second World War, has been it's pretention to play a role as the 'world conscience'. This would however be an unfair critique if directed at Myrdal's statement. His statement is in fact quite precise in its claim: that it was in Sweden's best interest to be the 'advocate of world interest', not that Sweden at all times would be able to follow such a course.

Myrdal's role in outlining the attitude of Sweden in post-war international affairs is generally underestimated. He was one of the principal participants in the Social Democratic Party's internal discussions when the international chapter of the party's post-war programme was formulated. Still more important – by his triple position as chairman of the Commission on Post-war Economic Planning, member of the direction of *Riksbanken*, Sweden's central bank, and as a member of Parliament he was able to develop the institutional channels by which the generally formulated aspirations could be consolidated.

Practical steps preparing a very active role for Sweden in the post-war reconstruction were actually taken. During the autumn of 1944 and the spring of 1945 the Swedish Parliament authorized *Riksbanken* to offer countries devastated by the war reconstruction credits to the impressive sum of 2.700 million Swedish crowns.[32] This sum was quite considerable: it exceeded the Sweden's actual currency reserves and was equivalent of 66 per cent of the 1943/1944 national budget. Not all of these credit limits were actually used but this gives a vivid illustration of the extent to which Sweden was prepared to play its role as 'advocate of world interest' in the post-war economic reconstruction of Europe.

In the minor but strategic post as Minister of Commerce in the Social Democratic government formed in 1945 Myrdal tried to apply these ambitions of a substantive Swedish contribution to the efforts of economic post-war reconstruction.

The reconstruction credits given to Finland in 1944 were essential for that country to avoid a situation of absolute starvation, and they enabled the Finnish economy to start paying reparation debts to the Soviet Union. In the immediate aftermath of the war vast material aid, in the form of pre-fabricated houses and essential goods, were delivered to neighbouring Denmark and Norway – and to the United Kingdom.

In less than a year Myrdal could proudly announce that Sweden had been able to arrange trade agreements with no less than 30 countries. In a situation where there was no generally accepted international currency system this was a feat in itself. It was only made possible by offering long term credits to Sweden's trading partners. After the armistice between Finland and the Soviet Union in September 1944, and during 1945, Sweden furnished neighbouring countries with credits amounting to 975 million Swedish crowns.[33] It was undoubtedly aid of considerable importance.

A financially important factor outside these credit agreements were the Anglo-Swedish Payments Agreement in March 1945, by which Sweden accepted the British pound as counterpart for its exports of steel and forestry products with a credit limit of 165 million Swedish crowns. This was done in a situation of non-convertibility of the pound and when it was obvious that the power of the pound was greatly undermined. It was in fact an important Swedish contribution to the British government's efforts to re-establish the pound sterling as an international currency.[34]

But the gestures that were most ostensibly noted politically were the important credit and trade agreements that Sweden made with Poland and the Soviet Union. Both were of strategic importance to Sweden. The Polish agreement centred on Swedish reconstruction aid in return for coal deliveries. The Swedish-Soviet Credit and Trade Agreement was from the outset framed on quite a large scale: Sweden granted one million Swedish crowns in credit for a five-year trade agreement.[35]

These trade agreements were clearly in line with Myrdal's ambition to open Sweden's trade relations in all directions, Eastward as well as Westward. It was also in line with the aim of using trade relations to facilitate a joint European reconstruction, transcending ideological differences.

Moreover – its complementarity with ideas professed within the US administration at the time should not be overlooked. The trade agreement was in fact in line with the attitude of the US representatives in the ongoing negotiations on the post-war arrangements of international trade. At the end of the London Conference on International Trade in November 1946 the US chief negotiator Clair Wilcox visited Stockholm to inform Gunnar Myrdal and the Swedish government of the conclusions of the conference (by virtue of its neutrality Sweden did not attend to the conference). On that occasion Wilcox voiced his full understanding and support of the newly signed Swedish–Soviet Credit and Trade Agreement as a measure of furthering international trade generally.[36] A gesture that was of great value to the Swedish government since the Swedish opposition parties had by then totally reversed their support for such an eastward trade.

The political landscape had indeed changed: the Swedish industrialists that were once protagonists for such a trade had by then been trapped in Safe Haven-negotiations in Washington, and were threatened with having all their US and UK assets blacklisted because of the industry's war time cooperation with Germany.

Tensions were rising between the Allies concerning the administration of Germany and the general attitude in the US and the UK towards the Soviet Union had grown considerably more suspicious. The once non-controversial Swedish trade agreement with the Soviet Union was suddenly regarded as dangerous by liberals and conservatives – as an ideological concession to communism and as an embarrassing burden for Swedish industry.

Their opposition drew considerable strength from the hawkish behaviour of those in charge of the Europe Desk in the US State Department. Quite in contrast with the US trade negotiators they (H. Freeman Matthews, Paul Nitze) argued that such a large Swedish commitment to trade with the Soviet Union would deprive the US economy both of Swedish products and of Swedish markets.[37]

The rapidity with which the domestic political scenery changed in Sweden in 1946 eventually became a stark reminder of Myrdal's far-sighted apprehension in his 1944 analysis of the post-war dangers: 'It is to be feared that our provision problems will be used upon us as thumbscrews to force us to go where we don't want to go.'[38]

Representatives of the Swedish exporting industries turned around under pressure from the US officials and backed away from trade deals, to save their US – and German – assets. Sweden – a small nation caught by American propaganda – was an easy prey to political pressures, transmitted via the newspapers of the political opposition.

Myrdal managed to push the Swedish–Soviet Trade Agreement through parliament, but when he wanted to protect Sweden against loss of its currency reserves, notably dollars, his warnings fell on deaf ears.

In early 1947 it was obvious that he had just as little potential to influence the Swedish minister of Finance as he had had in 1940. It is no wonder that Myrdal seized an opportunity to find a personal way out of the political impasse: in March 1947 he accepted the nomination to be Executive Secretary of the first regional UN commission to be formed, the United Nations Economic Commission for Europe (UNECE).

Myrdal's analysis of international affairs in 1944 is of importance as one of the principal inspirations for the subsequent Swedish post-war neutralism. With hindsight his cool 'realist' analysis was vindicated – Sweden was forced to go where it didn't want to go.

This analysis of the motives governing international politics tried to be less ideologically driven, more 'realist' – realism here is understood as a theoretical approach. The basic features of this analysis – coupled with a consistent fight for principles of justice, equal treatment and trade as a means of cooperation – were to characterize his international outlook throughout the following years.

In a period where the dichotomies of the Cold War era have subsided this outlook merits renewed attention.

In the Economic Commission for Europe and beyond: the functionalist civil servant preparing the future beyond stalemates

Gunnar Myrdal's nomination as Executive Secretary of the *UN Economic Commission for Europe* (ECE) in April 1947 removed him from Sweden's domestic struggles and catapulted him onto the international scene.[39] When he accepted this post his potential for promoting the kind of cooperation through trade he had established in Sweden was both weakened and widened.

From the beginning the high level of his ambitions was evident: in accepting the leadership of this organization, he brought with him his experiences from 1938–1942 as head of the Carnegie Foundation research project on 'The American Negro Problem'. It was at that time the second largest social research project so far conducted in the US, with a team of some forty scholars involved..

Of great importance was also his close companionship with David Owen, Assistant UN General Secretary and president of the ECOSOC (the UN commission heading all matters on economic and social affairs). Owen and Myrdal had met in political circles in Stockholm during the war, and Owen was the one who had pushed through Myrdal's nomination to the ECE. Through the close liaison they kept during Myrdal's term in the ECE, Myrdal could be sure that his initiatives would receive support in the higher echelons of the UN administration.

In less than a month Myrdal succeeded in assembling a highly qualified team of international officials. A large part of the 187 person strong staff came from the emergency institutions created immediately after the war,[40] but for all the new senior posts in the commission Myrdal insisted on making his own choice, following only the criteria of competence – and a certain balance as to the national representation. This insistence was a matter of principle: the ECE should not work as an intergovernmental organization but as an international one. This was not at all to the liking of some diplomats. The UK Foreign Office in London wanted to make their own decisions about whom should be dispatched to Geneva and who should not.[41] They had strong misgivings but could not stop Myrdal's appointment of Nicholas Kaldor as Head of the ECE Research Division, nor the appointment of the Russian scholar Mikhail Chossudovsky as Deputy Executive Secretary alongside Kaldor. The Foreign Office view was that nationals working within the UN should primarily see themselves as national representatives, thus applying considerations given by their governments. Myrdal insisted however that the overriding loyalty of the international officials should be towards the values and principles of the UN Charter and with the collective body within which they were working.

He did indeed manage to establish an undisputed authority within the ECE staff for this attitude – but at a cost: senior diplomats in the UK and US were wary of this independent-mindedness, fearing it might not be so easy to control.

The early months of ECE proved to be a baptism of fire. Europe was plagued with a severe economic crisis. The transportation system was in ruins, especially in Germany where the lack of coordination between the three occupation zones impeded economic recovery, and heating and food supply to a population on the brink of starvation. On the top of that the political dissensions between the former allies were growing. The Council of Foreign Ministers, held in Moscow in April, had ended in open discord. In a way the mere fact that the ECE was created in such a situation was a feat in itself. When the decision to create the UNECE was taken in March 1947 'it might very well have been the very last moment for such a decision to be taken'.[42]

The acuteness of the economic crisis in Europe was of no surprise to Myrdal. In his 'post-war manifesto' he had warned against the dire consequences of another Versailles Treaty – and the division and occupation of Germany was notably such a vengeance treaty. He had argued for an all-European effort at joint reconstruction, and as Minister of Commerce in Sweden he had tried to pave the way for such an initiative. However, most importantly he had been calling for a 'generous gesture' from the US – the only country able to provide the necessary means for long term recovery planning.

It was against the background of this newly established staff of high economic competence that Myrdal tried to make the ECE the coordinating body for the large post-war recovery aid that he knew was forthcoming from the United States.[43] He held high-level meetings with governments in Paris, London, and Moscow, and used his influence in Stockholm, Warsaw and Washington towards the same end.[44]

It was only in September 1947, after the first report of the Conference of European Economic Cooperation (CEEC)[45] had been scrapped by the US, that a different permanent European body was set up to coordinate the US aid, known as the *European Recovery Programme* (*ERP*).[46]

The geopolitical reasons behind the decision of the US, the UK, and France to set up the CEEC as an organization to rival the ECE will not be dealt with here.[47] However, it clearly signified the break-up of Europe into two separate political and economic spheres.

When it was clear that the pan-European approach to economic recovery favoured by Myrdal was no longer accepted, and that the ECE would be bypassed, Myrdal tried to ward off the geopolitical pressures on the ECE by giving the Commission two quite different tasks. The first one was to facilitate and strengthen trade ties among European countries. As a continuation of the so-called E-commissions set up by the Allies on transport and coal in 1945, all barriers impeding recovery and trade would be addressed on a technical level, in order to restore railways, ease bottle necks, and conclude bilateral trade agreements. This was a very difficult task after 1948, at the height of the Cold War. The embargo restrictions of the so-called Cocom[48] were applied to large sectors of the trade between eastern and Western Europe, and were at their height in 1952–1953. According to a comprehensive study, the proportion amounted to about 40 per cent of pre-war trade.[49] In spite of this, the network of trade representatives established by the ECE managed to play an important role in promoting intra-European trade. At a press conference in May 1954, Myrdal congratulated the ECE on the results of that year's conference:

> 133 bilateral meetings on trade issues were held between 25 countries.... The principal accomplishment of this conference was the fact it had enabled the experts to examine measures that could lead to an increase of east–west exchange in a spirit of mutual comprehension.[50]

The second task was an intellectual one: to provide quarterly surveys reviewing the economic problems of Europe, especially those of the least developed countries. These quarterly surveys were published independently, and they were not subject to any negotiation or comments by diplomatic channels.

By collecting essential data and providing the necessary analytical skills, the ECE staff would be able to exercise influence on public opinion and, hopefully, on governments. The first *Economic Survey* was published in early 1948. It demonstrated the expertise of the ECE staff to such an extent that, according to the British historian Alan Milward, it embarrassed the US authorities, since it 'was far more professional than the two volume report of the CEEC and constituted a scholarly critique of the bases of American economic policy in Europe'.[51]

According to some commentators the report addressing the steel over-production capacities in Europe even gave an important stimulus to the creation of the Coal and Steel Agreement in 1951.[52] Beyond matters of topical economic surveys the ECE also sought to address the wider issues of development theoretically. How to elaborate statistics to further the attainment of full employment? How to measure price development in the trade between underdeveloped and industrialized countries? How to develop measures furthering stability in the international economy? On all these issues the research team of the ECE played an important role.

The new, twofold orientation of the ECE – research surveys and trade facilitation – was characteristic of Myrdal's approach to problems of international economy in two ways. To begin with it asserted the ECE as an international organization, carrying the ethos of the UN charter, staying aloof from the Cold War division. Second it focused on international trade as a matter of cooperation and complementary relations, not on trade as competition and as a search for maximum cost efficiency.

In this way Myrdal was true to the 'functionalist' approach he had developed in his early writings on 'prophylactic social policy' in the 1930s. Once the needs were clearly identified, a rational discussion promoted by experts would demonstrate the need for radicalism in the practical solutions. It was in the bold application of practical and radical solutions that conservatism, social prejudices and outdated theories could be overcome.

In a situation dominated by ideological stalemates the ECE could offer the possibility of mutually beneficial trade between countries of differing political outlooks by enabling such a multitude of trade agreements in spite of the ideological barriers established by the Cocom procedures. By giving a level-headed analysis of economic problems and challenges in European countries East and West the ECE researchers provided a worldview which was far from the usual dichotomous ones.

This substantial contribution has been acknowledged by historians in a recent research project:

> Under Gunnar Myrdal's leadership, the ECE sought a middle way between the neo classical approach and the Marxist alternative, which

continental Western Europe translated into the so called 'social market economy' of the 1950s and 1960s. The Secretariat believed in indicative planning and State intervention to correct market failure and guide economic development. Gunnar Myrdal established, under the sole authority of the Executive Secretary, the publication of an independent annual report not negotiated by Member States: The Economic Survey of Europe. It proved to be a valuable source of information on Eastern European countries during the Cold War, not only for Western Europe, but for those countries themselves.[53]

Less known however are the circumstances leading to Myrdal's decision not to seek a renewed mandate at the ECE. When his fellow Swede Dag Hammarskjöld was appointed UN General Secretary in 1953 Myrdal initially had high hopes that he might be able to influence the general orientation of the UN in line with the universalist, all-inclusive approach favoured by the ECE and to increase the weight of what was then called the 'UN European Headquarters' in Geneva.[54] After all, Myrdal and Hammarskjöld had been in close collaboration in Sweden during the 1940s.

These hopes were however soon to be dashed. Even if Myrdal was held in high esteem by the ECE staff – Americans included – the US senior officials in Washington and New York were very wary about Myrdal and his attempt to steer a middle way in the East–West conflict. And Dag Hammarskjöld was in no mood to hurt the feelings of the US representatives.[55]

When Hammarskjöld – much to the opposition of the ECE staff and of Myrdal – tried to dismantle the ECE of its Transport Committee and relocate it to the UN Headquarters in New York, this lead to a clash between Myrdal and the US representatives at the ECOSOC meeting in September 1954. During this meeting Myrdal had been openly critical of the attempts by the US representatives to curb the measures proposed by the ECE to maintain East – West trade relations. This frankness had awakened the wrath of the US representatives who considered it to be beyond the limits of the mandate of a UN bureaucrat. In a subsequent letter to Myrdal, Hammarskjöld said he found the US criticism – only a mild version of the complaints he had heard – to be 'constitutionally fully justified', and argued that it was also damaging to Hammarskjöld personally, when he was trying to secure the position of the Secretary General: 'I have to proceed with caution – also in relation to the friendliest governments – in my efforts to widen and consolidate recognized rights.'[56]

Even if Hammarskjöld eventually had to concede on the practical issue – the Transport Committee remained in Geneva – it was then obvious to Myrdal that any hopes of a special relationship with the Secretary General must be abandoned. It was furthermore obvious where the balance of power lay within the UN organization: Geneva was not the 'European centre' of the UN but only its auxiliary.

Other factors of a personal nature might have been of importance. It is nevertheless a rather safe conjecture that this deception was of importance, when Myrdal decided not to seek a renewed mandate as Executive Secretary of the ECE, but instead gradually reoriented his attention back to the academic and intellectual field.

Looking back at the ten years Myrdal spent at the head of the ECE it must be regarded as quite an accomplishment. In years of heated Cold War disputes Myrdal managed to maintain the integrity of the organization, to steer it free of great power politics and to maintain and develop links of technical and commercial cooperation between European countries across the East/West divide.

That such links were maintained – in an adverse political climate – was valuable later on when Myrdal's wartime friends Bruno Kreisky and Willy Brandt found it possible to inaugurate the new 'Ostpolitik'.

In a sense, being one of the very few remaining European organizations which incorporated all Europe's countries on an equal basis, the ECE was true to the ideals of the 'Kleine Internationale' assembled in Stockholm during the war years in the forties. The final conflict between the General Secretary of the United Nations and the Executive Secretary of one of its regional organizations finally illustrated clearly a major and persistent dilemma for the United Nations: that of how to maintain its integrity when its headquarters are located at the heart of the world's most powerful nation, the United States?

Wrestling with issues of trade theories and development: from Columbia to Cairo

It was thus with the backdrop of yet another political deception that Gunnar Myrdal decided once again to change the area of his activities. Or rather, that the Myrdal couple jointly decided to change careers: in 1955 Alva Myrdal was promoted to Swedish ambassador to India in New Delhi, and they decided that he should follow her here there, as soon as his obligations at the ECE permitted.

Returning to his studies in social sciences was perhaps not such a big step: during all the ECE years Myrdal had been involved in studies of European regional development via the quarterly publications of the ECE Surveys. But the invitation to speak on trade and development issues provided the impetus to broaden the research questions.

We will now turn to the development of his ideas as witnessed by his magnum opus, four works on questions of trade and development: *An*

International Economy (1956), *Economic Theory and Under-developed Regions* (1957), *Asian Drama* (1968) and *Challenge of World Poverty* (1970).

Invited as a keynote speaker to the celebration of the 200-year anniversary of Columbia University New York in 1954, he embarked on broadening his research on trade and development issues, now expanding it from the European region to of the world and the international economy as a whole. What were the determining conditions of development and growth in the poorer regions, where the majority of the world's population lived? He expanded his Columbia lectures into a comprehensive analysis of problems of the international economy and published *An International Economy* in 1956.[57]

Myrdal's point of departure in this book was that there existed a paradoxical contrast between developments in 'advanced industrial countries' and the trend on the larger international scene, especially in underdeveloped countries. In the former case, the trend was towards national integration and establishing a welfare society, in accordance with 'the Western world's inherited ideals of liberty and equality'. In the latter case, the trend was in the opposite direction, towards disintegration and increasing disparities.

As he had in *An American Dilemma*, he again concluded with a call for moral decisions as a solution: it was only by paving the way for a more equal distribution, for a 'welfare world', that educated opinion in the advanced countries could live up to their own publicly assumed ideals of 'liberty' and 'justice'. This, in essence, was formulated from the standpoint of an economist situated in a core country.[58]

Using Myrdal's own critical tools one might say that his use of the term 'underdeveloped countries' showed a value-laden bias. Although formulated in universal terms, referring to Enlightenment values of freedom and equality as the basis for international integration, this term postulated development as a linear process, with 'industrially advanced' countries at the top of the ladder.[59]

However, when approaching the practical problems of overcoming this international paradox, the 'core economist' changed camp: he went south. He was already a long standing critic of the conventional free trade theory paradigm and its assumptions of mutual benefits. In *Varning för fredsoptimism* he had argued that political factors skewed the prices of raw materials in a way disadvantageous to colonized countries, and the research report, produced by among others his friend Nicolas Kaldor at the ECE, confirmed this analysis.[60]

In his 1956 analysis of the predicament of 'underdeveloped' countries he referred to yet another source of influence: 'the remarkable series of studies by Prebisch and his fellow researchers at the Latin American equivalent of the ECE, the Economic Commission for Latin America (ECLA)'.[61]

He specifically emphasized Prebisch's repudiation of 'the false sense of universality in the "general economic theory"' and regarded it as 'a tenet of these nations' spiritual revolt for independence and development.'[62]

To avoid the 'false sense of universality' given the 'free trade' theory dominant in the negotiations on international trade within the GATT rounds Myrdal proposed that underdeveloped countries should 'tackle the subject deliberately from the viewpoint of their own interests'. This call for a deliberately partial view was not surprising – as Myrdal had argued earlier – values and ideologies are inescapable elements in economic theories. This should hold for the international economy just as much as for the national.

In his subsequent analysis of the internal development problems of the 'underdeveloped' countries[63] there was a new and strong emphasis on the important role of institutions. Against any mechanistic understanding of market economies, Myrdal developed an institutional explanation for the apparent stability of 'welfare economies' in the industrially advanced countries.

In fact, it was only through the expanded and regulating role of the state, based on egalitarian values and with the support of strong labour organizations, that broadly based social growth had been possible in these countries.

On the international level, however, such countervailing forces were absent – so far. True to his dynamic and Wicksellian understanding of economic processes, Myrdal criticized the assumptions of comparative advantage in the doctrines of free trade: international trade would lead to increasing welfare gaps instead of mutual advantages, if left to the influences of technology and investment margins alone.

Although critical of what he saw as ECLA's 'narrow industrialization strategy',[64] he highlighted the need for rapid industrialization in these countries, as well as their right to let their developmental needs determine their trade policies.

But changes in the rules of the international economy alone would not be sufficient to create possibilities of development for the under-developed countries, according to Myrdal, domestic changes were crucial.

In line with his earlier argument on economic policy in Sweden, he also advocated that radical domestic reforms, above all land reform, would be equally necessary as a change in trade relations between developed and underdeveloped countries. Myrdal clearly spelled out that these reforms would be hard to accomplish, since 'modernizers' in the state would meet resistance from landed interests, as well as from 'economic enclaves' benefiting from actual trade relations.

According to Myrdal, the world's hope for a peaceful solution of the economic and social problems triggered by gross inequalities depended on two interrelated changes: first 'that the underprivileged nations succeed in joining forces effectively', and secondly that 'as the present power vacuum is thus filled a greater equality of opportunity is brought about'.[65]

For all his moral appeal to the liberalism of the 'Western world', his main hope for change expressed in this book lay in the growing solidarity between 'underdeveloped' countries. It was in the hope of stimulating these aspirations that Myrdal continued his work. In 1956, at the height of Egyptian nationalism and the emergence of the Movement of Nonaligned Nations, he was invited to Cairo to hold a series of conferences, from which he later published *Economic Theory and Underdeveloped Regions*.[66]

In this book, he dedicated a central chapter to a frontal attack on the Heckscher–Ohlin trade theorem on factor price equalization, arguing for a broader framework of analysis:

> To define a certain set of phenomena as the 'economic factors', while keeping other factors outside the analysis, is a procedure closely related to the stable equilibrium approach. For it is precisely in the realm of those 'noneconomic factors', which the theory usually takes as given and static that the equilibrium approach is most unrealistic, and where instead circular causation is the rule.[67]

In Myrdal's view there was a 'circular and cumulative causation' pushing towards greater inequalities within countries, as well as between them: 'the main idea I want to convey is that the play of the forces of the market normally tends to increase rather than decrease the inequalities between regions'.[68]

In this analysis he expressly drew upon the research of the ECE, notably drawing two conclusions:

> the first one is that in Western Europe disparities of income between one region and another are much wider in the poorer countries than in the richer ones.... The second conclusion is that while the regional inequalities have been diminishing in the richer countries of Western Europe the tendency has been the opposite in the poorer ones.[69]

The reasons why the 'unrealistic' assumptions of free trade benefits still dominated were of an ideological order. He claimed:

The equilibrium approach, with its strong ideological connotations, comes in then as convenient and opportune. For while a realistic approach, recognizing the predominance in social developments of circular causation having cumulative effects, gives arguments for central planning of economic development in an underdeveloped country and large-scale state interferences, the equilibrium approach, because of the inherited ideological connotations, leads to laissez-faire conclusions.[70]

However, these conditions were soon to change, as Myrdal hoped that

the changed situation in the world ... and the appearance on the stage of the learned discourse of a host of new participants from nations which have until recently been kept passively submissive and mute are bound to represent the beginning of a revolution also in the social sciences, widening our horizon and radically redirecting our thinking. Out of this mighty process should also emerge a more realistic and relevant economic theory.[71]

This call for 'a more realistic and relevant economic theory' was a widely shared attitude within the United Nations held by the representatives of Latin America and the representatives from former colonial countries. By the early 1960s, the impact of decolonization was being felt through the new leverage of the 'developing countries' at the UN's General Assembly, where they engaged in forging new and higher levels of global solidarity. In July 1962, a Conference on Problems of Developing Countries was held in Cairo. This marked a first joint initiative of countries from all three regional groups – Asia, Africa, and Latin America. The 'Cairo Declaration' called for an international conference on 'all vital questions relating to international trade, primary commodity trade and economic relations between developing and developed countries', within the framework of the UN.[72]

That claim was brought to the UN, where an ECOSOC resolution in August 1962 supported the convening of a UN Conference on Trade and Development (UNCTAD). This could be considered as an attempt to resume the close ties between trade and development present in the International Trade Organization charter, a connection left defunct but not forgotten.[73] These countries managed to have the UN General Assembly in 1961 to pass a resolution to convene a Conference on Trade and Development issues. The conference, originally conceived as a one-off conference, managed to set up the UNCTAD as a new permanent UN body.

With Raùl Prebisch as its first Secretary General the hopes were high that UNCTAD would provide a countervailing force able to change the agenda of world trade to one explicitly linking trade to the needs of the lesser developed countries. It managed to establish a general commitment from the industrialized countries to increase their development aid to the level of 1 per cent of their GDP, a level advocated by Swedish representatives. This success turned out to be rather hollow since the major industrialized countries refused to give a time table for this ambition to be achieved, and it has been a source of discontent ever since. Still more damning was the refusal of the industrialized rich countries to agree on any more comprehensive and binding measures to change terms of trade. The next step was that the developing countries proposed within UNCTAD that a new set of trade rules should be put in place, a comprehensive programme called the 'New International Economic Order'.

It was actually endorsed by a UN General Assembly. But when Prebisch tried to translate it into binding resolutions at UNCTAD's second Conference in New Delhi in 1968, it fell through because of the opposition from the major developed countries. The developed countries were not interested in giving concessions to the 'Third World' countries. And these countries in turn proved to be a group too weak and divided to provide effective opposition. Frustrated by this failure Raùl Prebisch decided to resign from the organization and to return to his regional base, the UN Economic Commission for Latin America (ECLA/CEPAL).

Gunnar Myrdal, who at the end of the 1950s had pinned such high hopes on the emergence of a theoretical revival coming from the Third World movements, also shared Prebisch's deep disappointment at the fate of UNCTAD. In 1968, he characterized the UNCTAD meeting as 'almost a complete failure'[74] quoting the speech of Prebisch on 'the lack of political will' of the dominant countries. Arguing the need for 'regional cooperation with joint planning', Myrdal blamed the failure on splits between the 'underdeveloped' countries, and their inability to overcome them. But he also blamed the refusal of industrially advanced countries to offer concessions, be it on commodity prices or those of agricultural and manufactured products. Myrdal concluded: 'The majority of the developed countries, with the United States in the lead, are now intent on putting UNCTAD on ice.'[75]

The decade he had spent on trying to change the 'free-trade' agenda in international economy thus ended with yet another proof of the impotence of international organizations when powerful interests were at stake.

Modernization and the internal impediments to development: South Asia in focus

One of the main points in *International Economy* had been the highlighting of the internal impediments to change. The populous Indian continent with its millions of poor was a glaring example of the deep divide between 'rich lands and poor', of the increasing gap between rich welfare states and underdeveloped countries, grappling intractable development problems. In a way, India was the 'free world's' bad conscience.

When Alva Myrdal was appointed Swedish ambassador to India in New Delhi in 1955 this gave Gunnar Myrdal the opportunity for a new vast research project: to study the development issues in South Asia. A project which eventually lead to the publication of *Asian Drama: An Inquiry into the Poverty of Nations.*[76]

When analysing the mechanisms in the international economy in his earlier books economic patterns had been the focus for Myrdal. When embarking on his journey into the realities of South Asia, it was by returning to the broad sociological approach of *An American Dilemma* that he tried to answer his own questions.

When addressing the so-called 'Negro problem', Myrdal had put the governing elite's own values in question by contrasting their 'American Creed' and their failures to live up to them. In *Asian Drama* Myrdal was using the value of 'modernization' in much the same way: to what extent were the governing elites, local and external, living up to values contained in that metaphor?

True to his trans-disciplinary approach Myrdal's work on development issues in South Asia developed into a sprawling labyrinth of local cultural attitudes, diversity of farming conditions, the role of middlemen, landed aristocracy and civil servants.

As an exercise in trans-disciplinary work *Asian Drama* is one of impressive comprehensiveness.[77] Its 2,800 pages sometimes lack the synthetic clarity of *An American Dilemma* but in its richness it gives a broad understanding of the diversity of South Asian cultures and societies. As such it is still a powerful antidote to the Western – colonial – view of the South Asian 'other'.

In the end *Asian Drama* provides a panorama of social, cultural and economic factors impinging on – and mostly restricting – the efforts of the national governments in India, Pakistan and Sri Lanka to further economic and social development.

Myrdal did not come empty-handed to grapple with these issues. As a participant in a parliamentary commission on 'population questions' he had contributed a lengthy analysis on the structural problem of Swedish agriculture, further expanded in his book on agricultural issues in Sweden.[78]

The gist of his argument had been that a reliance on family-based unity of production should be the basis for a much needed thorough 'rationalization' (introduction of modern methods in farming). This attitude – largely the official Swedish agricultural policy of the post-war years – had a double facet: on the one hand the state should strongly discourage farming units that were too small to make a proper living for independent farming families, on the other an organization of distribution cooperatives should be supported in order to protect family farmers against efforts of industrially run farms to squeeze them out. The urge for an extensive land reform runs deep in *Asian Drama.* And Myrdal's insistence on the value of family-based units of production have proved their value, for instance in China. But of course the general conditions, not least the power relations within the chains of distribution, were totally different in India from those prevalent in Sweden. Where Sweden had a majority of independent farmers, with their own political representatives and their own cooperatives of distribution – the Indian farmer, when independent, was regularly in the hands of moneylenders and middlemen.

Another area where Myrdal went back to his early debates in Sweden was the question of the link between development and population growth. But here the link was reversed. In Sweden the tendency of the population to decrease presented itself as a danger for social and economic development, in South Asia it was the too rapid population growth that undermined the viability of the small farms and increased the flight into vast urban areas. Here a transition to a more slow growth pattern was a general desire – but in the absence of true and radical land reforms a relatively large number of children remained the only tangible retirement assurance available for the poor in the countryside.

While insisting on the need for fundamental land reforms there was also a new insistence in Myrdal's text on the role of education in changing the cultural attitudes that stood in the way of modernization. If changes have to come from below these changes had to be considered over a longer time span. But even in this field the vast social inequalities tended to pervert efforts: too much was given to secondary and higher education which was used by the elites, rather than assuring that primary education was made available for all.

We can see how Myrdal translates his analysis of economic theories onto the social field: the general mechanism is not a tendency towards equilibrium but a circular and cumulative causation. Economic inequalities in Western, industrialized and capitalist societies tended to create vicious circles of unemployment if unchecked. Much in the same way the vast inequalities in South Asian societies tended to block development and perpetuate mass poverty.

Despite a lot of good intentions among the elites Myrdal saw 'a conspiracy of the upper layers of society' stifling or diverting all attempts at modernization. Another important change in Myrdal's view on development problems in the 'underdeveloped' countries was his attitude regarding the role of the state in the transformation process. When working on these problems Myrdal was in close contact with India's governing elite. Alva Myrdal was not only Sweden's ambassador to India, she was also friends with Jawaharlal Nehru, the Indian Prime minister. The Myrdals knew to what extent Nehru and his administration were carried by ideals of modernization, they knew and appreciated the Indian government's ambitious economic planning for the industrialization of India.

When making local studies, the glaring contrast between the bold visions of the New Delhi planners, and the inertia and petty egoism of the local administrations, became evident to Myrdal. India was not ruled by a Weberian state, imbued with rationalism. Grappling with the problem of politics and local governments Myrdal developed the concept of a 'soft state', that is a state were political decisions to a large extent are diluted and diverted on its way to implementation. It is to Myrdal's great credit that he so clearly and so early identified the problem of corruption. How corruption perverted any coherent effort at political reform, and at the same time it undermined Myrdal's own conception of how development and modernization should come about. To what extent could such a 'soft state' be used as a tool for development? This was a crucial question for an author who had assiduously been preaching the need for state planning in underdeveloped countries.

In a retrospective analysis in 1978 he suggested that even if the ideals of modernization and equality often were given prominence a 'forceful pressure from below' would be needed for these ideals to have a force of their own: 'no upper class group have ever abstained from their privileges only because of good intentions and ideals'. A pressure he then saw as rather distant, given the 'dominant pattern of mass passivity in the underdeveloped countries'.[79]

When Myrdal embarked on his large study of social conditions in South Asia and the impediments to development it was with a methodology similar to the one used in his study of race relations in the United States. He was using the officially proclaimed ideas as a tool with which to measure the attitudes and actions of ruling groups. In the case of Southern Asia it was the ideal of 'modernization' that was the common creed of the planners. It was also an ideal shared by Myrdal himself. However, on his research sessions on the Indian countryside, he gradually became aware of the vast distance between the everyday conditions of the farming population, and the material and intellectual worlds of the planners in the central Indian administration. The relative importance of cultural and institutional impediments was therefore much more emphasized in his conclusions in *Asian Drama*.

Modernization must be seen rather in a longer haul than the actual five-year planning models. It had to rely on a change of attitudes that would take generations to accomplish.

Poverty was singled out as a problem in itself, not only as a matter of inequality. Even if poverty in part was a symptom of the larger, structural problem and a symptom of the power structures – it was also a problem in itself. It created vicious circles. The population problem in South Asia was, as already mentioned, the opposite of the problem he and Alva Myrdal had discussed in Sweden. Overpopulation in India was a problem in itself, undermining the resources of families and providing the basis for below-subsistence wages. It had to be reined in by birth control measures.

Consequently the role of increased access to education was seen both as a tool for changing family structures via family planning methods, as a way of heightening the ability of the poorer members of the farming population to take advantage of new technological possibilities. And also to increase their political awareness so as to push for political reforms, especially land reform.

In his analysis of the development problems in South Asia Myrdal took a major step towards a thorough and complex institutional analysis expressed by his dynamic analysis of the problem as a 'circular and cumulative causation'.

Challenge of world poverty: back to the American Creed?

The publication of the mammoth *Asian Drama* was followed by praise for the comprehensiveness of the study and the acuity of its critique of the misplaced use of Western economic concepts in analysing the realities of Asian societies. There were however, also voices in 1968 which criticized Myrdal for having too few proposals which offered solutions. This was the subject of *Challenge of World Poverty* (1970), characterized by Myrdal as 'a summary of the political conclusions scattered in various parts of Asian Drama'.[80]

At the beginning of this work he got an invitation to gives a series of lectures at Johns Hopkins School of Advanced International Studies in the United States in 1969. The time and the audience gives a clue to the orientation of *Challenge of World Poverty*: it was addressed to a forum of US liberals after five years experience of the 'War against Poverty', proclaimed by the US President Lyndon B. Johnson.

The greater part of the book was devoted to the need for internal reforms in 'underdeveloped' countries. Emphasis was on the broad social questions: equality, agriculture, population and education. He spelled out the inadequacies of current policies: technological progress in agriculture and land reforms had primarily benefitted the wealthier in the countryside, not the poor rural masses that needed it most. The expansion of education had likewise been more suited to the needs of the already literate. As regards the question of corruption and on the dysfunctionalities of the 'soft state' Myrdal mentioned the aggravating role of outside forces: 'private Western business interests are commonly deeply engaged in corrupting politicians and officials in all underdeveloped countries'.[81] In these areas Myrdal spelled out several measures to be taken. But who should carry them out? On this account he presented a stark dilemma: the 'middle classes', the rural elites, the educated were living in conditions far from those of the vast majority of people and had other concerns, while the masses were mostly 'passive, apathetic and inarticulate'.

The hope Myrdal harboured was a moral one:

> People are usually not simply hypocritical, still less cynical, when in their daily strivings they compromise their ideals. The intellectual elite in an underdeveloped country usually do believe they should identify themselves with the nation. The upper class is privileged; but historically it has been, and is today, the bearer of egalitarian tidings. Its moral situation can be said to be weak if ever it is challenged by events.[82]

In analysing the international context Myrdal reiterated the critical analysis developed in *Rich Lands and Poor* (1957): international trade was not diminishing but increasing inequalities: 'the underdeveloped countries have been and are still largely at the mercy of the play of market forces'.[83]

The problem was further compounded by the commercial policies of the developed countries: 'The commercial policies of the developed countries are almost systematically rigged against the efforts of underdeveloped countries to rise out of underdevelopment.'[84]

Partly as a consequence of this Myrdal noted the rising debt burdens of the underdeveloped countries as a growing problem: 'If present trends continue all the gross inflows of capital will be swallowed by the outflows, including debt services, sometimes in the early 1970s.'[85]

The faith Myrdal had expressed 13 years earlier in the rising demands from public opinion in underdeveloped countries was now almost totally dissipated. The UNCTAD session in New Delhi in 1968 was characterized as 'almost a complete failure', the underdeveloped countries had not managed to formulate any radical demands and when it came down to concrete issues they were crippled by internal splits.[86]

Where did that leave his primary audience, the liberal elites of the industrially advanced countries?

The gist of his message was a moral call: 'only by appealing to people's moral feelings will it be possible to create the popular basis for increasing aid to underdeveloped countries as substantially as needed.'[87]

Against those who thought this was unrealistic he wrote: 'Frankly, I believe it is unrealistic and self-defeating to distrust the moral forces in a nation.'[88]

Arguing his point of the power of moral concerns in politics Myrdal used the Marshall Plan as an example of an 'almost boundless generosity of the United States to the West Europeans'.[89] Even if the government chose to motivate the Marshall programme by Anti-Communism the main motivation of the American people, according to Myrdal, was 'much more the positive one of sympathy and solidarity with nations which were badly off'.[90]

In the actual situation Myrdal was pinning most of his hopes on the new orientation of the World Bank, formerly the International Bank for Reconstruction and Development. He felt that its new emphasis on population control, educational advance and agricultural progress was well motivated. He even saw the Bank intervening in the national policies:

> Indeed, now that the Bank is increasingly becoming imaginative and willing to exert its influence in the underdeveloped countries for progressive policies, it could go one step further and actually be prepared to use some of its resources for aiding underdeveloped countries to carry out land reform.[91]

Despite all his earlier misgivings about the commercial policies of the developed countries Myrdal hoped that the Bank's new approach would also be guiding the aid policies of individual developed countries: 'The vision opened up before our eyes would be the close cooperation between the Western developed countries and the progressive forces in the underdeveloped countries.'[92]

In fact, instead of being major and dominant actors in a power structure based on inequalities, Western governments might be a crucial outside factor favouring social reform in the underdeveloped countries. This moral call was most specifically directed towards public opinion in the United States. In the political conclusion of *Challenge of World Poverty* this was especially clear. Referring to 'the grim failure of the Vietnam involvement and several other imperialistic adventures, particularly in Latin America' Myrdal wrote, with allusion to passages in *An American Dilemma*:

> I refuted the idea that even then I found common in America, namely that financial and military power could be a substitute for the moral

power of earning the good will of all decent people in the world. Without followers, the leader is no longer a leader, but only an iso- lated aberrant. And if he then is strong, like America, he becomes a dangerous aberrant, dangerous for himself and the world. The leader- ships the world now needs from the United States must spring from clear thoughts, rational analysis, and devotion to peaceful living and development.[93]

Under the leadership of Robert MacNamara, former US Secretary of Defense, the World Bank was, at the beginning of the 1970's, moving away from development goals focused on overall macro-economic growth to make 'poverty alleviation' its main focus. This new focus also entailed a new attitude, with more direct intervention. Helping people rather than helping governments often meant bypassing the governments, using the World Bank's own experts to conduct local farming projects. This was a change Myrdal basically favoured.

Challenge of World Poverty starts with a reminder of the welfare paradox signalled in Myrdal's earlier books on the international economy: while the welfare states in industrially advanced countries were reducing inequalities, the divisions between those countries and the underdeveloped regions were continually growing. This in itself posed a challenge for public opinion in the 'rich lands': not only from a moral point of view, but also in view of social and political consequences. The industrially advanced countries must provide underdeveloped countries with the aid necessary for them to tackle the poverty problem.

In the early sixties Gunnar and Alva Myrdal had been among the fore- most protagonists in creating a comprehensive Swedish development aid programme. In this regard it is interesting to see how Gunnar Myrdal changed his opinion of how this aid should be oriented. His early belief was that development aid should furnish capital needed to trigger eco- nomic development, somewhat in the line of the gradual stages of growth as experienced in the history of the industrialized countries. When he singled out poverty as the central issue Myrdal was obviously – and once again – in tune with discussions in the United States.

As we have seen, *Asian Drama* presented strong arguments as to why it was relevant to single out poverty as a problem of its own, creating vicious social circles in the Asian countryside. But making it the central problem also on the international scene had another effect: it obscured the structural flaws of the international economy that Myrdal had so succinctly analysed in his earlier work *International Economy* (1956). The emphasis on the need for internal reforms in the developing countries was fully justified, but these demands could be – and were – interpreted as a softening of the critique towards the role of advanced countries in international economy. Poverty was after all, mainly their problem, not ours. Myrdal himself argued against such an interpretation, but the fact is that the structural effects of neo-colonialism received sparse attention, and the attempts of third world economists to raise the question of a new international economic order was treated witha lack of enthusiasm.

In *Challenge of World Poverty* Myrdal is a long way from the trust expressed in his Cairo lectures regarding the capability of economists from Third World countries to develop new theoretical tools to guide the international economy.

The appeal to the moral motivations of Western elites may have been justified but it obscured the way in which these ideals were moulded by structural circumstances. The ease with which the World Bank's orientation changed, from being the benevolent lender of loans for agricultural projects, to the hardnosed enforcer of the Structural Adjustment Programs in the 1980s, bears witness to this weakness in Myrdal's approach. The method of taking professed ideals of ruling elites at face value and contrasting them with policies actually pursued can undoubtedly have its merits. But the scientist must also be able to evaluate the relative weight of those ideas in what motivates the actors. By unreservedly taking the official, altruistic values of the US liberal elites for granted – in fact transposing his own values onto this liberal elite – Myrdal's own perspective on development issues had changed. In an article, written together with Andrés Rivarola, comparing the development of his ideas with those of Raùl Prebisch, I have characterized this development as that one where the 'core' economist, disappointed with the elites and the economists in the countries of the 'periphery' returns to a 'core' perspective on world development issues.[94]

Introducing ecology into economics: the UN Conference on Human Environment 1969 and beyond

If his conclusions in *Challenge of World Poverty* were not on a par with his earlier theoretical critique of dominant paradigms, in 1972 Myrdal still showed his capacity for understanding the need to reformulate our way of understanding the world. In view of the importance of the ecological dimension signalled in the introduction, Myrdal's thoughts in 1972 on that matter merit close attention.

The post-war years had witnessed a rapid growth of productivity in the agriculture of the industrially advanced countries, particularly the United States. This had been accomplished by technological advances, new seeds but also by an intensified use of chemical pesticides. Rachel Carson's

Silent Spring, published in 1962 illustrated the dangers of this development in a way that alerted public opinion in Sweden as well as elsewhere.
Myrdal, who as economist and social scientist had been one of the most
outspoken in arguing the virtues of economic growth and economy 'at full
steam', came to re-evaluate growth as general solution and to reflect on
necessary limits to growth. He was very early aware of the concerns of
natural scientists and opinion makers on the dangers of uninhibited growth
to environment.

When addressing environmental issues Myrdal acknowledged his
indebtedness to the warnings of two Swedes, the demographer Georg
Borgström[95] and the geographer Hans Palmstierna.[96]

The public debate caused by their contributions was current when
Sweden was invited to host the first UN Conference on Human Environment in 1972. In connection with this conference Myrdal gave a lecture on
the 'Economics of Improved Environment' that drew considerable attention.[97] In this lecture he once again proved his ability to understand the
breadth of human challenges in a new era.

On that occasion Myrdal embarked on an area that was new to him – that
of the ecological constraints on economics – and since the difficulties and the
dilemmas he then exposed to a large and increasing degree are still with us, it
is relevant to outline some of his main arguments in more detail.[98]

At the outset he emphasized the vast extent of the dangers evoked, and
insisted they must have far-reaching consequences for the current way of
thinking:

> The anxieties now expressed by biologists and other natural scientists
> working on the world's ecosystem concerning the impending deple-
> tion of irreplaceable natural resources – water, energy, some crucial
> metals, and arable land – and the pollution of our environment – air,
> water, land, animals, indeed our own bodies – should rightly have
> important consequences for development planning in developed and
> underdeveloped countries and primarily for economic theory both on
> the macro- and micro-levels.
>
> Looking at the development of agriculture and population growth
> from a historical perspective there were reasons why the 'optimism',
> the belief in unlimited and continuous growth was so dominant. The
> gloomy forecasts of Malthus[99] had not come true, he noted. Instead
> the preceding century had been one of historically unprecedented
> growth and gradually rising living standards, even for the poorer sec-
> tions of the population. Nor had fears about impending scarcity of raw
> materials materialized – the reality had been the opposite, a
> continually good supply of raw materials. In fact, Myrdal believed this

ample supply had been one of the great problems for people in under-developed regions, their development prospects had continually been hampered by over-supply and low prices of their products. But there were crude historical factors behind the growth pattern in agriculture:rapid technological advance in agriculture as well as industry, from the middle of the nineteenth century, the huge increases of food imports to Britain and Western Europe generally from the emigrant settlements in the areas of the New World where the natives were not so numerous and could be killed off or segregated in various ways and still later the spontaneous spread of birth control.

To a considerable degree, the development of Western-oriented agricultural production thus been built on injustices committed towards the native populations in the 'New World'. But this state of affairs had changed after the Second World War and with 'the hurricane of liberation from the colonial power system that after the Second World War swept over the globe'. The underdeveloped countries were now raising their demands for development, and they were basing their planning on the same faith in the unlimited space for growth.

It was also possible to explain why fears of the depletion of raw materials had not yet come true. Myrdal advanced two factors, the discovery of new supplies, particularly of oil and metal-ores, and technological inventions making it possible and economically profitable to economize or replace the use of some scarce raw materials. But the fact that depletion had not yet occurred couldn't be taken as an argument concerning the future, Myrdal said:

> From my studies, though naturally inexpert, of what my colleagues in the natural sciences have more recently reported I have however become convinced that we must finally recognize and prepare for the fact that there are limits to growth whose component elements all follow an exponential curve.

The notion of growth elements following an 'exponential curve' is especially important to note – it refers in itself to the dynamics of tendencies he had evoked in social science, that of the 'cumulative causation'. In this context it also refers to the relationship between man and nature.

After some reservations about the uncertainties involved in all predictions his judgment of the severity of the ecological danger is stark:

> The reservations about the uncertainty of all forecasts I have piled up merely imply that the future, when uncontrolled growth comes up

against serious limits is somewhat indeterminate, but essentially within the range of only one or at most a few generations. In any case, with the unprecedentedly rapid and still accelerating growth of the world's population which we must now take as fairly certain to continue for many decades we shall invite catastrophic developments, unless we are prepared now to introduce and enforce various restraints and deflections of production and of consumption and indeed, our ways of life.

The new challenge that Myrdal conjures is profound indeed: if 'catastrophic developments' are to be avoided we will have to enforce changes in the basic economic functions of society. To meet this new situation he believed that nothing less than a profound overhaul of economic sciences was needed. This overhaul would have to be accomplished largely against the profession of economists: 'As usual economists are in a mighty way supporting the ideology and psychology of continuous and unlimited economic growth'

In what ways was it necessary to reconsider economic theory in the light of the ecological challenges? Myrdal singled out 'two traits in modern economic theory that reflect this accommodation to prevalent thinking and which consequently have to be given up, or altered in a radical way. The first was the concept of gross national product, the second trait which had to be changed radically was the analysis of markets: 'fundamentally economic analysis has retained its character of being carried out in terms of a price formation in competitive markets'.

Discussing the concept 'Gross National Product'[100] he noted that it was 'flimsy' when applied in developed countries and very much more so in underdeveloped ones:

> Several of the many thousand categories of income and cost elements are thus defined in a grossly arbitrary way: some elements are not included at all in the calculation of the GNP. And any attempt to introduce ongoing depletion of pollution into the calculation of the GNP must fail because of the gross uncertainties I have alluded to.

He discarded attempts to define a broader concept of 'social utility' as 'doomed to remain on a level of useless speculation'. Not only did the concept lack any 'reliable quantification of things deemed desirable or harmful', moreover it lacked any reasoning of the interrelationships between different factors: 'The almost total absence of quantitative knowledge about the coefficients of the interrelations between the various factors determining the movement of the social system as a whole.'[101]

Myrdal, true to his understanding of the 'circular and cumulative' character of chains of reaction, here shows the complexity of the matter: not only do we lack reliable quantitative knowledge about effects of specific factors, we also lack a proper understanding of the interactions they produce.

This absence of reliable quantification should however not be an excuse for inaction, nor should it make worried scientists succumb to unwarranted quantification (as Myrdal argued was the case with the Rome Report). What was needed was instead, an acknowledgment of the limits of our quantifiable knowledge: 'a hard simple thinking aware of the limitations of what we know'.

The second general trait that had to be given up or radically altered was the understanding of the functioning of markets. According to economic theory:

> the preferences of all concerned are expressed in aggregate form by their demands and supplies. Production and resource allocation are steered by relative profitability. With regard to depletion and pollution the fact is however the very heavy discounting of the future at the present time represented by interest and profit rates. This implies that the time horizon becomes much narrower than should be accepted by our collective societies which must consider developements decades and centuries ahead. When as has happened economists argue that as resources become scarce the cost of these resources will rise so that depletion is avoided they are not taking into account the fact that this reaction does not come early enough so as to be rational and sufficient in order to avoid depletion.

Here is, succinctly formulated, a telling verdict of the fundamental incapacity of a market-ruled economy to cope with environmental problems: uninhibited actors on the market are driven by immediate returns leaving the costs to other people to pay later. And the price correction mechanism, when it eventually arrived, would not prevent catastrophes, since it would not come early enough. Earlier in this book we presented Myrdal's critique of the incapacity of neo-classical economic theory to deal with the dimension of time. This critique now comes back with a vengeance: modern economic theory was not capable of dealing with the ecological demands of long-term sustainability.

The challenges for economic policy when intervening were by consequence tremendous. Myrdal considered previous effects of protectionist measures usually to have been rather marginal:

The new restraints and deflections rationally motivated by considerations of long-term effects of the trends towards depletion and pollution but infringing upon people's impulses to follow their individual short-term preferences must in comparison stand out as radical'.[102]

This thoroughgoing critique of the ineptitude of current economic theory ended in a somewhat surprising conviction:

I feel sure that economic science will increasingly be able to lay the foundation for such radical planning which may be necessary to meet the pending dangers of depletion and pollution. It will imply however such alterations in our approaches that we would have the right to talk about a 'new economics'. To what extent such a development of our theory would influence government policy is another matter however.

How would such a 'new economics' be established? Myrdal was pessimistic about his own profession, it was not to be expected that they should be in the vanguard for such a fundamental change in society and their own science: 'The main pressure will in the future years, as well as up till now, have to be exerted by those natural scientists who are studying the ecosystem.[103] The changes necessary in economic theory thus had to come from forces outside the professional economists. The young economist's conviction of the force of an 'immanent' rational critique of erroneous economic theories is no longer there. The new economy has to be built from outside the established discipline of economics.

In addressing the environmental problem at large Myrdal was differentiating between two kinds of problem, the administrative problem and the political. The administrative problem was about the mix between price policies and controls and about how to apply controls so that policy decisions really become effectuated.

The political problem was however the more serious of the two:

How is it possible to move from a general awareness by the public of the dangers ahead, and of the policy-deciding instances acting on behalf of the public, to a preparedness to impose the controls needed? This would ideally imply a centrally imposed and enforced planning of almost all economic and indeed all human activity.[104]

This 'ideal' solution is however never seriously considered. Instead he continued the more general discussion on how to get public opinion to endorse the changes needed, first on a global perspective, then also on national levels.

On this question he started by affirming the close link between environmental and social concerns. To Myrdal it was obvious that those who were most immediately threatened by the environmental crisis were the great majority of people living in underdeveloped countries. He gave two reasons for this, climate factors and population growth. The densely populated agricultural areas were particularly defenceless against the destructive forces of climate, of pollution and sometimes of the depletion of resources. And above all population growth appeared to Myrdal to be 'the key factor in the environmental problem'. On a general level he argued the both availability of resources and pollution in these countries in many ways were a function of the density of population.[105]

The trend towards increasing inequalities in most underdeveloped countries – a trend that he had thoroughly discussed in his earlier works – was likewise a factor that made him foresee a rather grim development in the decade ahead: 'increasing underutilization of labour and as a result great misery among the rapidly swelling masses in the rural and urban slums'.

This inequality was a problem not only within underdeveloped countries, it also had to do with the way international trade was working. As an example of the 'sinister consequences' of the actual international trade in resources and near raw material products, Myrdal referred to a study by Georg Borgström:

> underdeveloped countries are continually exporting large quantities of high-quality, protein-rich food products to make overeating possible in the affluent developed countries, and sometimes to provide food for dogs and other domestic animals, or to be used as fertilizers. But even aside from that type of export from underdeveloped countries which deprive them of primary products from land and sea that they would very badly need for themselves for feeding their largely undernourished and malnourished population which is now rapidly increasing, the fact must be spelled out that the small minority of people in developed countries appropriate and use for their own production and consumption an entirely disproportionate and steadily increasing part of the world's resources. One broad inference is that any hope that the living levels in the underdeveloped world would ever even approach those in the developed countries would presuppose a radical increase of their use of irreplaceable resources.[106]

The last part of his lecture was devoted to questions of policy and power. Having underlined the inequality aspect of the environmental situation he insisted that any serious discussion about environmental problems had to tackle the distributional issues: 'Who has the power over resources? The

disregard of this issue makes much of the now common brave and broad pro-
nouncements utterly superficial and misleading, indeed meaningless.'

Gunnar Myrdal was known to be tempted by provocative frankness. To
make his point against superficial prouncements clear, he noted that, 'it is
now customary to say that the 20 or 30 percent of the part of mankind
living in the developed countries now for their own use, dispose of some
80 percent or more of the world's natural resources'.

He then went on to denounce what he saw as a lack of consequence in
the environmentally aware public opinion in developed countries:

> Particularly with the now growing awareness of their threatening deple-
> tion this would in turn necessitate acceptance of substantial lowering of
> living levels in developed countries. I see no sign of such a thought,
> even among the most ardent advocates for the necessity of taking a
> global view of the use of resources and certainly not in the announced
> aid policies in any developed country. My main point, however, is the
> purely logical request that any discussion of threatening depletion of
> resources in global terms, if it shall not remain on a level of general and
> unclear phrase-mongering must define a stand on the distributional
> issue. Is the assumption made that in the interest of greater equality in
> the world there should come to be a more fair distribution of resources
> between developed and underdeveloped countries in order to make pos-
> sible a corresponding speeding up of their development? Or is instead
> the assumption made that the present proportion appropriated by
> developed countries is going to be upheld and even gradually increased
> with their rising levels of living, including the large imports of resources
> from the underdeveloped countries? The second alternative of status quo
> on the distributional issue is apparently taken for granted. This should
> then in all honesty be stated. And the word 'global' should be used with
> more care, spelling out that tacit assumption.[107]

The distributional issue was thus for Myrdal at the heart of the matter:
who shall bear the costs for defending environment? The question of
inequality as a major obstacle to progress was once more reaffirmed.

After this quite pessimistic diagnosis about the willingness of people in
the advanced countries to accept a more equal distribution he went on
explaining the many mechanisms hampering policy measures also on the
national level in advanced industrial countries. Even when there was a
public awareness about the environmental problem there would be a
reluctance to accept the consequences: 'Besides entailing costs policy
measures being taken to preserve and improve our environment will regularly restrain people's freedom to do what they please.'

Taking the question of 'automobiles' as a special case he guessed that cars would eventually become safer and less polluting, but that was only part of the problem:

> All big cities are severely overcrowded by automobiles. Not only is the air polluted by exhausts but the transport situation is in a mess, without any government or municipal authority having felt it possible to restrict effectively the use of automobiles. The owners and would-be owners are everywhere by far the biggest political party. And in no developed country, as far as I know, has it proved politically possible to get the car owners to pay the full costs, including also the heavy investment costs for roads and adjusting cities to the cramming of cars in the streets, the costs implied for all delays caused to people in the cars and on the streets, the costs for policing the traffic, and the very heavy public and private costs caused by the accidents, not to speak of not paying for the pollution of the air.[108]

By this example alone he clearly demonstrated the inadequacies of a GNP/GDP-concept. When measuring GDP these costs will appear only as growth factors. In this example he also highlighted the weakness of the concerns for general interest in confronting the pressure groups motivated by particular interests.

He was sceptical towards current declarations of good intent stressing the resilience of old habits:

> General declarations in favour of 'a new style of life' ... have a general appeal to any public. But the accustomed 'style of life' has a great power to survive, particularly in a competitive economy, where every group is bent upon defending and raising its income and levels of living. Almost our entire institutional structure and our attitudes are geared to growth of the old kind.

Moreover there was a general problem with measures defending the environment: 'It it true that in the long run these costs may be profitable and result in higher productivity. But initially the costs are heavy. The costs come first, far ahead of the returns.'[109]

The political problem was further compounded when Myrdal looked at the international arena:

> Coming then to the still broader problem of a world-wide cooperation to protect and improve environment it is difficult to see the prospects to be bright. We have behind us a number of conspicuous failures to

reach inter-governmental agreements in fields where common interests should be very strong and of even more urgent character.[110]

The areas Myrdal referred to were the negotiations on armaments control and aid for the development of underdeveloped countries. The latter area – the aid for development – was characterized as 'decreasing quantitatively and its quality is deteriorating', a fact 'largely hidden to the general public by a gross falsification of the statistics'.[111]

One main problem in confronting the environmental problems on a global scale was the lack of appropriate institutions:

> I see no political mechanism, through which action could be taken for preserving resources. We have not a world government, still less a world government having power to enforce planning on a world scale of the use of resources. What we have are matrixes for government cooperation. This would do, perhaps, but only if they were used more effectively for inter-governmental agreements on important issues such as those now concerning the United Nations Conference on the Human Environment.[112]

Any hopes that Myrdal logically shared on the need for world planning were thus far away, the major political institutions were still the national governments and the agreement they might establish. Given such a difficult political climate it was quite a modest ambition that Myrdal spelled out for the moment:

> I believe it is prudent that we should feel happy if the Conference can preserve the momentum in the awakening of interest in the environmental problem, set up a permanent agency for continuing the work, build a substructure for carrying it out in the regions and sub-regions under UN auspices, and in addition perhaps outline a few badly needed treaties in regard of intergovernmental cooperation in preventing pollution of air and water.

In retrospect that was a fairly realistic guess: the following UN conferences on environmental problems have become steadily more concerned with dealing with the ecological impact of present patterns of economic growth, treaties on special issues have been reached, but at the same time the dimensions of the ecological threats have continually widened.

The major part of the dilemmas Myrdal pointed to in this speech are still relevant. His critique of dominant economic theory could be written today: GDP is still the most common tool used in economic policies in spite of its profound inadequacy in dealing with ecological problems. Despite the obvious failures of the market mechanism it is still in many quarters looked upon as a panacea for a smooth escape out of the ecological crisis. Myrdal's insistence on the paramount role of the distributional issue, on the problem of global inequalities as a major impediment to any solution of the environmental problem is likewise fundamental today. The only difference on that account is perhaps that the speed of economic development in Asian countries has sharpened the conflict.

It is in his way of addressing the political problem, the problem of how to change public opinion, that his approach has undergone the most notable changes. Where the younger Myrdal felt convinced that, once a 'rational' solution was presented dilemmas could be transcended, the elderly scientist framed the question differently. How can general interest prevail when confronted with powerful pressure groups defending particular interests? How can citizens be prepared to accept the immediate costs and restrictions of liberty when returns are far away?

The question of time horizons is likewise treated in a different way. The younger Myrdal, understanding the vital role of expectations in the economy, outlined long-term planning perspectives where the interests of modern industrialists would converge with those of the labour movement. The elderly scientist could present no such attractive alternative. Nor could he advance any new 'creed' that would have had a compelling appeal to ruling elites. The task of convincing people to act immediately to avert a possible danger in the future – a problem that still had not made itself felt physically – was a much more arduous one. It was clearly colouring the rather 'prudent' ambition of his analysis.

Myrdal, the internationalist disappointed: the urgency and impediments to international cooperation

At the end of the war Myrdal – despite his warnings – had an optimistic view on the overall tendencies in international economy and politics. He was part of the radically liberal trend in the world's new leading power, the United States. He was at least partly sincere in 1946 when he characterized the ongoing negotiations of how to organize international trade relations as a 'demand for international economic planning on a giant scale'. When he accepted the leadership of the UN ECE he was for a time convinced that this commission would be charged with organizing the aid of the European Recovery Program.

When he looked back on his tenure in the ECE ten years later his hopes were much more subdued. In two articles in a Swedish newspaper, he summarized his reflections on the role of international organizations and the shortcomings of international cooperation. Reflecting on the prevalent mood towards the end of the war he noted:

> The peoples at home and on the other side of the war front were promised a future welfare world and as basis for this a reliably organized peace and and intensive economic cooperation within the framework of the many international organizations then established.... Measured against this, judged in the light of these expectations there can be no other conclusion than our international organizations on the economic field have been failures.[113]

The reason he provided was that it had both to do with the post-war situation and the paradoxes of the ulterior development. Acknowledging these very high hopes he admitted that the current period was one of disillusionment. In part this was a natural reaction. The planning for the post-war years had a necessary psychological function: 'People had to believe that the world would be radically remade when the war against the fascist countries had been won.... All wars however bring in their wake intensified nationalism, and so did this one too.'[114]

His judgment on what had been accomplished was indeed very severe. Among the specialized UN organizations it was only the regional commissions that were recognized to have at least accomplished 'a modest start of cooperation between the countries in the region concerning a large number of practical and technical problems'.

Of special interest is his strong critique of the central organization of the United Nations:

> The UN General Assembly and its Economic and Social Council has been fora for discussion and propaganda but hardly ever been used for their main statutory tasks, initiating and coordinating international cooperation on broad lines in the economic and social spheres. During the last years especially the last organ, the ECOSOC, has sunken down to an almost scandalously low level of irrelevance.

This was indeed a very harsh critique of the action of the accomplishment of fellow Swede Dag Hammarskjöld as UN General Secretary and shows the depth of their conflict in 1954.

How could this have happened? First of all, the promises made when establishing the international organizations of the UN were given in an 'opportunist' moment giving hope to their populations, meaning to the war being fought: 'the idealists and the planners had an open field for their strivings'.

Opportunism should not be understood here in a pejorative sense: The expectations then cultivated, the promises then given were by no means empty propaganda. They corresponded to sincere expectations and honest resolves. It is interesting but somewhat worrying to read today what was said, written and published 12–15 years ago. Even knowledgeable people with sound judgments were then firmly believing that the organizations then prepared and established would be efficient tools for international cooperation. They were actually safely hoping that these organizations would develop in such a way that they later on might provide the framework for a true world community, a kind of democratically run welfare state.

Myrdal himself being one of these knowledgeable people, one might ask why these expectations were not fulfilled: why were international organizations still so inefficient? The main reason given by Myrdal in this set of articles was the ascendancy of 'narrow and unwise nationalism'. And in the prevalent climate of the Cold War he argued that it would be wrong to put the blame the Russians and the Soviet bloc. The project of an International Trade Organization was aborted and the International Monetary Fund was a failure – these were failures of the Western governments since the Soviet bloc remained outside these negotiations.

Myrdal placed the main responsibility at the level of the national governments:

> The real reason why all international organizations only very much less than expected have come to function as efficient organs for real economic integration is that the governments in the individual countries have not allowed this to happen. Above all they have not been prepared to accept the limitations of their freedom to orient their national economic policy that this would have entailed.

The dominance of the mechanism of 'narrow and unwise nationalism' was moreover supported by imbalances on the domestic scene: 'In all countries there are organizations of different kinds, political parties and pressure groups exclusively to defend certain special interests. But in no country is there a powerful organ to defend the country's stake in the general world interest.'

However Myrdal refused to give up hope for the future. The main reason for his optimism was 'the fact that a continuing disintegration was such an enormously expensive luxury for all'. He also enumerated some basic assets on the credit side of the international organizations: they compiled statics and produced research of value for political economists and governments. Also the mere fact that they continued to exist, and that by doing so, they represented 'the diplomacy of the future'. In spite of the shortcomings he had had detailed, Myrdal was hopeful: 'In fifteen or twenty years I believe that the international organizations will be able to present quite a different balance account.'

However even this subdued optimism was to prove exaggerated. In Myrdal's final comprehensive summary of the state of international cooperation, at a lecture held in 1977, he was more the worried world citizen than the assumed optimist. His topic again addressed the dilemma of: 'the increasing interdependence between the established national states but the failure to solve common problems which have piled up precisely because of the increased interdependence.'[115]

Once again he highlighted the strength of national interests. In part this was a side-effect of the deepening of the welfare states:

> everywhere the scope of policy measures decided upon and put into effect by, and within, the national states has continually become much greater in recent decades. It also means that people's interests become introverted to what can be attained within the individual state. Compared with these strivings, carried out by everyone individually and through professional organizations and political parties within the frame of the national state, endeavours for international cooperation are difficult to experience in a concrete way. They come to stand out as abstract ideals, not easily incorporated into the daily experiences of living in a consolidated national state.

Thus development of the increasing role of the national states – much favoured by him – had the reverse effect of strengthening the introversion of their citizens. Another new obstacle to international cooperation was the accrued role of transnational corporations as actors on the international arena due to changes in technology and in the organization of production: 'the technological development in transports and communications have lead to a growth of international trade faster than that of the production as a whole, implying ever closer links between the national economies' and 'a parallel and equally rapid developments in techniques of productions and of management in commerce, industry and partly in agriculture has generally given big corporations competitive advantages.'

Their dominance had accelerated and they were largely escaping political control. Countervailing forces such as the trade unions, present on the national arenas, were largely absent internationally.

Instead of being able to show instances where there were promises of an increased role for the international organizations (IGOs) he could only show new obstacles. The dilemma presented in 1957 – that is the disparity between on the one hand the need for increased international cooperation and the mutual benefit that could be derived from this, and on the other the overall process of disintegration and increased inequality – this dilemma had become even starker by 1977. In fact Myrdal presented the situation here as one with even deeper structural roots than before. The problems present in 1957 were now compounded by the contours of the looming environmental crisis (the question of the depletion of non-renewable natural resources, the question of dangerous pollution). Even the main asset in 1957 – the deepening of welfare states – was now undermined by the 'stagflation' crisis.[116]

The main danger in 1957 – that of a large scale war between major powers – had been avoided, but the problem of arms control remained acute. Instead of presenting a positive balance sheet demonstrating the accomplishments of the international organization Myrdal gave an in-depth structural analysis of the urgency for such a co-operation.

He highlighted four areas where the deepened mutual dependence demanded international cooperation: that of arms control, non-renewable resources, pollution and the stagflation crisis. And finally – as a fifth world problem – the question of international equality concerning living standards, and ultimately the distribution of resources between developed and underdeveloped countries, actualized in the demand from developing countries at the UN General Assembly for a 'New International Economic Order'.

True to his analysis of the interdependency of problems he stated that none of these problems could be resolved separately from the other: 'Our failure to deal with them in international cooperation will have repercussions on how all other problems will present themselves. These repercussions represent what I usually characterize as circular causations with cumulative effects.'[117]

Values and shortfalls in Myrdal's outlook on international affairs

Commenting on the legacy of Gunnar Myrdal, John Kenneth Galbraith has said: 'he defines the time and the century, including what has gone wrong'. In fact the time span between Myrdal's post-war manifesto in 1944 and his sombre remarks on the inefficiency of international organizations in 1977 very much characterizes the hopes and the failures of the post-war period.

Taking his outlook in 1944 as a vantage point I think the development of Myrdal's thinking on international economy is best understood as carrying the values and hopes of the US radical liberalism of the war years.

More than the ideals explicitly professed – those of Enlightenment, rationalism, equality, modernization – it was also structured by the perspective of the United States as the rising world hegemon, even if it was with a heterodox and critical eye. This perspective was a factor behind the continued – and continuing – relevance of Myrdal's ideas: they intervened in the dominant discourse of the times, showing its biases and inconsistencies. It was also a factor behind some of the shortcomings in his ideas, since all perspectives paint realities in a partial light – as Myrdal readily would have conceded.

At the end of the war Myrdal stood out as a staunch defender of Sweden's national interests in a chaotic post-war situation, a defender of 'world interest' firmly based in political realism and sceptical about the great power politics of the United States. At the head of the UN Economic Commission for Europe he was the international civil servant bridging the Cold War divide and trying to defend the ethos of the UN as an international organization against political pressures, again mainly from the US administration. When he returned to science it was first by adopting the perspective of the disadvantaged, 'under-developed' countries that he continued his pre-war critique of the methodologies and inconsistencies of dominant neo-classical economic theories, while extending them to a forceful criticism of free trade theorems and narrowly economic solutions on social problems.

He still stands out as one of the main heterodox economists in his early critique of free trade theorems and the unwarranted use of unrealistic models in analysing economic and social dynamics. His early critique of the GDP concept and the flawed and unsubstantiated statistics used are also guiding remarks which are still relevant. His insistence on the need to break out of the cage of economics, to adopt transdisciplinary approaches in addressing international economic and social problems is likewise, wise – if challenging – advice.

Beyond being a rigorous heterodox economist he is above all the moral critic par excellence of the state of world affairs. It had been a highly efficient approach to use the methodological device of the 'American Creed' in addressing the inconsistencies and prejudices of the US liberal elites, in challenging their self-image, and in making them confront their own responsibilities in 1944. To transpose this methodological device into the international arena, as he did in *Challenge of World Poverty*, had been less so. Partly this had to do with the difference in contexts. In 1944 US liberalism was strong both domestically and abroad, projecting itself as Europe's saviour from the Nazi terror. In 1970 it was morally isolated by the Vietnam War and preoccupied with contenders both in industrial countries (Japan, Germany) and in its Latin American backyard. The idea that the well-being of people in the Third World – the 'underdeveloped countries' – would be an equally pressing moral concern for US liberal elites and US citizens in general, as the elimination of domestic racial discrimination was flattering to the self-image of the US liberals that he spoke to, but it was hardly a realistic assumption.

This does not mean however that the relevance of Myrdal's moral call should be belittled. In basing itself on the ethos of the Charter of the United Nations – itself largely a product of US liberalism – it transcends the borders of the United States and implies a moral duty to the governments of all the UN member states. In that sense there is a clear link between the UN Declaration of Human Rights and Myrdal's call on world opinion to address the challenge of World Poverty. This call has been heeded by specialized UN organizations such as the UN Development Program. Its work on developing several Human Development Indices, incorporating gender and environment issues in its yearly Human Development Reports is paving the way for the more realistic social and economic statistics Myrdal called for. These kinds of statistics were also used when the Millennium Development Goals were formulated in 1995. As a moral measuring stick they still play an important role in shaping the agenda of international affairs.

But exactly how important is that role? When progress is made, to what extent is it due the moral choices of powerful nations? When do moral concerns take precedence over their economic interests? And to what extent is the progress that can be observed primarily the result of national policies pursued by individual developing countries?

The development of the debt crisis for the poorest countries – the Least Developed Countries (LDCs) and especially the most vulnerable among them, the Highly Indebted Poor Countries (HIPCs) – clearly showed that narrow economic concerns of the richest industrial countries in the latter decades of the twentieth century took precedence over moral concerns. The debt crisis of LDC's was in the first instance largely a by-product of the drastic shift in interest policies of the US in 1979–1980 due to domestic concerns. In the United States and also in Great Britain interest rates were drastically increased to stifle current domestic inflation. The fact that this change in monetary policy similtaneously drastically increased the debt burden of poor countries didn't enter into the picture at all. And once the debt crisis was acute the main concern of the lenders in the industrial countries – and of the World Bank and the International Monetary Fund – was to secure the debt servicing, with no consideration for rising poverty in countries most seriously hit. When progress has eventually been made – in countries as diverse as China, Brazil and Venezuela – it has been the national policies pursued that have made the difference.

In what marks Myrdal's manifesto in international as well as in national affairs, *Varning för fredsoptimism*, he wrote that the time needed 'burning hearts but cool brains' and he often celebrated the need for realism in analysing international affairs.

There can be no doubt of his 'burning heart', of the persevering internationalist attitude, of his call for cooperation and compromise between ideological opponents even at the height of the Cold War, of his insistence that mutual benefits of resolving common problems in cooperation would always be larger than any short term gain by egoistic behaviour – and thus of his adherence to radically liberal values. In his insistence on the overarching importance of attacking inequalities in international arenas he is moreover one of the most vibrant defenders of the ideals contained in the Declaration of Human Rights.

But as for 'cool brains': to what extent was he really a realist in his analysis? We have discussed the lack of realism in his appeal to the moral concerns of the US public opinion. To a certain extent this was due to the existing intellectual framework: although in his questioning and criticizing of the Cold War divide there was no doubt on which side he positioned himself. Sometimes the reader wonders whether Myrdal really was sincere in *Challenge of World Poverty* in 1970 – or whether he was only arguing instrumentally, to convince his US audience. Did he really think that the Marshall aid meant that the United States showed an 'almost boundless generosity' towards countries in Western Europe, an aid without strings attached? This was not the position he himself held in 1948, when Cold War dynamics were in full swing. In 1970 he rightly denounced the 'passivity and apathy of the masses' as one fundamental impediment to necessary egalitarian reforms in underdeveloped countries. One of the few examples he mentioned to the contrary was the case of Vietnam. But why was it then such a 'hateful experience' that 'the awakening of the masses, and their becoming conscious of their interests, happened in a constellation where they find themselves projected into a movement of national Communism'?[118] It is understandable that he, 'a student in the great liberal tradition of Enlightenment', would have preferred another way but why should it be 'hateful' if peoples in underdeveloped countries followed their own ways to a more egalitarian developement? When talking about Sweden's interest in the post-war years he clearly spelled out the force of nationalism in creating cohesion around a national project: so why should this be refused to other peoples, under characteristics dictated by their own particular history?

For all Myrdal's courageous critique of the US intervention in Vietnam – his treatment of Vietnamese nationalism shows the Cold War limits of his

Enlightenment values. It is for instance remarkable that he still voiced hopes for the land reform the US wanted to implement in Vietnam in 1970.

This value premise made him less open to discuss different national development paths that would have been 'rational' from his own point of view.

There is also a certain one-sidedness in his appeal to moral concerns in international affairs. True, one might accept that it is 'unrealistic and self-defeating to disregard moral concerns of a nation'.

Moral concerns do matter, but how much? The degree of political realism in his 1944 manifesto is often lacking in his later works. Here Myrdal's rationalism is underdeveloped. As a social scientist he discusses the difference between reason and rationalization. People want to be rational and consistent, he says. Sometimes they use rationalization to explain and defend attitudes that are not consistent with their professed values of more general character, as 'expediencies of the occasion'. Normally values of a more general character take precedence over lower-degree values and rationalizations: 'In Western culture people assume, as a general proposition, that the more general and timeless valuations are morally higher.'[119]

But when does a powerful nation recognize that its professed values – such as 'saving the free world' or the 'Alliance for Progress' in Latin America – are rationalizations of short term egoistic interest rather than ideals of higher value? When do moral concerns take precedence?

The role of power relations and power balances in making dominant powers recognize compromises, settlements or adjustments is poorly developed by Myrdal. In a way this is surprising since when Myrdal was explaining the development of the Swedish welfare state he described it as a matter of balance between industrial interests and the labour movement. The need for national counterweights in the underdeveloped regions to the weight of industrially advanced countries is addressed in *Rich Lands and Poor* but much less so in his later work.

Notes

1 Her articles in various newspapers were published as A. Myrdal, *Stickprov på Storbritannien* (Stockhom, Natur och Kultur, 1942).

2 Misgeld, K., *Die 'Internationale gruppe Demokratischer Sozialisten' in Stockholm 1942–1945. Zur sozialistischen Friedensdiskussion während des Zweitens Weltkrieges* (Uppsala: 1976).

3 It was in connection with this group that Alva and Gunnar Myrdal also met a young British diplomat stationed in Stockholm, David Owen. A relationship that later was to become quite important when the latter became deputy General Secretary of the United Nations.

4 It is a sign of the times that when Myrdal's American publisher wanted to go ahead with the editing in 1945 Myrdal declined, too many things would have to be reviewed. At the time Myrdal was heavily burdened with his work in the Post-war Economic Planning Commission.

5 Myrdal, *Varning för fredsoptimism* (1944), p. 16.

6 Ibid., p. 11.

7 Ibid., p. 284.

8 Ibid., p. 267.

9 Ibid., p. 274.

10 Ibid., p. 345.

11 Ibid., p. 347.

12 At this moment Alva Myrdal had been the most prolific writer of the couple, with a regular political column in the social democratic daily *Morgontidningen*, and with books on public debates in Great Britain and the Allied post-war planning. Apart from public appearances in 1940 it was only after the completion of his work on *An American Dilemma* and upon returning home in 1943 that Gunnar became a prominent participant in the Swedish public debate again.

13 Myrdal, *Varning för fredsoptimism* (1944), p. 11.

14 Ibid. p. 69.

15 Ibid., pp. 104–111.

16 Ibid., p. 281.

17 Ibid., p. 204.

18 Ibid., p. 206.

19 Ibid., p. 194.

20 Ibid., p. 207.

21 Ibid., p. 208.

22 Ibid., p. 309.

23 Ibid., pp. 278–279.

24 Ibid., p. 291.

25 Ibid., p. 315.

26 Ibid., p. 313.

27 Ibid., p. 317.

28 Ibid., p. 293.

29 Ibid., p. 301.

30 Ibid., p. 300.

31 Lewis L. Lorwin, *Det andra världskriget och dess ekonomiska följder* (Stockholm, Bonniers, 1942). Reviewed with praise by Gunnar Myrdal in 1942, describing the author as 'one of the founders of the so-called institutional school'.

32 A summary of credit allowances in the Government's *Proposition 1945:295*. The discussions around the post-war credit allowances are detailed in Appelqvist (2000), pp. 182–185.

33 Summary from *Riksbanksfullmäktiges särskilda protokoll* (The confidential Record of the Central Bank of Sweden), on 17 October 1947. Appelqvist (2000), pp. 262–263.

34 Efforts that eventually failed in 1947, with a considerable loss for Sweden's currency reserves.

35 It is of interest to note the early history of this agreement. It was initiated by a request from Swedish industrialists in 1940, at a time when the Non-Aggression

Pact between Germany and the Soviet Union was in place. Swedish industry's interest in the Soviet market was thus quite compatible with its close collaboration with the German war effort. After the German attack on the Soviet Union this initiative was put on hold and was not re-activated until 1944, then by acting Minister of Commerce Bertil Ohlin, leader of the Liberal party. By then argument of the Swedish industrialist was somewhat different: it was to avoid being cut out of the promising Soviet market by US firms that prompted the Swedish government to act. A full account of the history of this agreement is presented in Birgit Karlsson, *Handelspolitik eller politisk handling. Sveriges handel med öststaterna 1946–1952* (Göteborg: *Ekonomisk-historiska institutionen*, 1992).

36 Substantiated in Appelqvist (2000), pp. 386–387 by diplomatic cables and newspaper interviews.

37 Negotiations between Hammarsköld and the US State Department officials in Appelqvist (2000), pp. 389–395.

38 Myrdal, *Varning för fredsoptimism*, p. 347.

39 A detailed account of this nomination is given in Kostelecký, Václav, *UN Economic Commission for Europe: The Beginning of a History* (Göteborg: Landsorganisationen, 1989). Also in Ö. Appelqvist: 'Rediscovering Uncertainty: Early Attempts at a Pan-European Post-war Recovery', *Cold War History*, Vol. 8, No. 3 (2008), pp. 327–352.

40 European Central Inland Transport Organization (ECITO), European Coal Organization (ECO) and Emergency Economic Committee for Europe (EECE).

41 His choice of Nicolas Kaldor, instead of the Foreign Office choice of Harry McNeill, was viewed with displeasure by Bevin according to Kostellecky (1989).

42 Kostellecky (1989), p. 36.

43 Örjan Appelqvist: 'A hidden duel: Gunnar Myrdal and Dag Hammarskjöld in economics and international politics, 1935–1955', *Stockholm Working Papers in Economic History*, Vol. 2, 2008.

44 Cay Sevòn, *Vägen till EuropaSvensk neutralitet och europeisk återuppbyggnad 1945* (Helsinki: Suomen historiallinen seura, 1995), pp. 168–175.

45 The official name of the Paris conference, later to become the Organization of European Economic Cooperation.

46 Alan Milward, *The Reconstruction of Western Europe 1945–1951* (Cambridge: Cambridge University Press, 1987), pp. 69–89.

47 The arguments of the chief actors are discussed in 'Rediscovering Uncertainty: Early Attempts at a Pan-European Post-War Recovery'. Note above.

48 The Cocom was the 'Coordination Committee', a semi-official coordination between the US State Department and government officials in Western countries, to establish a list of products considered to be of military significance.

49 Gunnar Adler-Karlsson, *Western Economic Warfare 1947–1967: A Case Study in Foreign Economic Policy* (Stockholm: Almqvist & Wiksell, 1968).

50 'Myrdal dresse le bilan de la conférence commerciale est-ouest', *Le Monde*, May 1954.

51 Milward (1987), p. 84.

52 Proceedings of the Conference in 2005 of the United Nations Intellectual History Project (UNIHP), p. 93.

53 United Nations Intellectual History Project (UNIHP), *Reflections on United Nations Development Ideas: Proceedings of Conference on 24 January 2005 in Geneva – From Development to Governance*, p. 93.

54 According to Myrdal's archivist, Stellan Andersson, Myrdal told him that he himself was one of the three names on the final short list for the nomination.

55 This development is detailed in 'A hidden duel: Gunnar Myrdal and Dag Hammarskjöld in Economics and International Politics 1935–1955'; cf. note above.

56 Hammarskjöld to Myrdal, 'Personal and Confidential', 10 August 1954, Vol. 6.1.009. 23.1.2.34 *AGM, ARAB*.

57 Gunnar Myrdal, *An International Economy: Problems and Prospects* (New York: Harper, 1956).

58 We are referring here to the manner in which 'dependency' theorists such as Raúl Prebisch are characterizing the main division in the world economy as being a structural one between 'core' countries – industrially and financially dominating – and the 'periphery' of lesser industrialized countries, more dependent on exports of primary products.

59 On the other hand, it is fair to note that Myrdal himself regarded the more usual term 'developing countries' as a euphemism, hiding their actual state of affairs. The current distinction between 'developed' and 'developing' tries to avoid a pejorative denomination.

60 *Post-War Price Relations in Trade Between Under-developed and Industrialized Countries* (New York, 1949, E/CN.1/Sub.3/W.5). United Nations, National and International Measures for Full Employment: Report by a Group of Experts appointed by the Secretary-General of the United Nations. B. Ronald Walker, Chairman; J.M. Clark, Nicholas Kaldor, Arthur Smithies, and Pierre Uri (Lake Success, New York, 1949).

61 Myrdal (1956), p. 222. ECLA is better known by its Spanish acronym CEPAL, Commisiòn Economica para América Latina.

62 Ibid., p. 223.

63 G. Myrdal, *Economic Theory and Under-Developed Regions* (London: Duckworth, 1957). Also published in the US as *Rich lands and Poor* (New York: Harper & Row, 1957).

64 Myrdal (1956), p. 228. The argument is, however, not developed much further here.

65 Myrdal (1956), p. 319.

66 G. Myrdal, *Economic Theory and Under-Developed Regions* (London: Duckworth, 1957.

67 Ibid., p. 157.

68 Ibid., p. 24.

69 Ibid., p. 26. This is an explicit reference to Ingvar Svennilson *Growth and Stagnation in the European Economy* (Geneva: UNECE, 1954).

70 Ibid., p. 159.

71 Ibid., p. 162.

72 John Toye and Richard Toye, *The United Nations and the Global Political Economy: Trade, Finance and Development* (Bloomington, IN: Indiana University Press, 2004), p. 187.

73 The post-war negotiations on international trade had produced a charter for such an organization, the ITO, at a conference in Havanna, Cuba in 1948 but since the US Congress refused to ratify the convention what remained was a negotiation procedure, the General Agreement on Tariffs and Trade (GATT).

74 G. Myrdal, *The Challenge of World Poverty* (London: Allen Lane, 1970).
75 Ibid., p. 309.
76 G. Myrdal, *Asian Drama: An Inquiry onto the Poverty of Nations* (New York: Twentieth Century Fund, 1968).
77 In order to create the infrastructure needed for this project the *Institute for International Economy* was founded in at the University of Stockholm, Sweden in 1962. Many of its researchers, notably Ellen Boserup, played an important role in assisting Myrdal on this research project.
78 G. Myrdal, *Jordbrukspolitiken under omläggning* (1938).
79 G. Myrdal: 'Behovet av reformer i under-utvecklande länder', *Världspolitikens dagsfrågor*, 1978, p. 10.
80 G. Myrdal: 'The need for reforms in underdeveloped countries', lecture given in August 1978. Quotes from *The Essential Gunnar Myrdal* (2005), p. 210.
81 G. Myrdal, *The Challenge of World Poverty: A World Anti-Poverty Program in Outline* (New York: Pantheon Books, 1970), p. 249.
82 Myrdal (1970), p. 77.
83 Ibid., p. 284.
84 Ibid., p. 294.
85 Ibid., p. 291.
86 Ibid., p. 301.
87 Ibid., p. 368.
88 Ibid., p. 369.
89 Ibid., p. 337.
90 Ibid., p. 340.
91 Ibid., p. 261.
92 Ibid., p. 262.
93 Ibid., p. 385.
94 Ö. Appelqvist & A. Rivarola: 'Prebisch and Myrdal: Development Economics in the Core and on the Periphery', *Journal of Global History*. Vol. 9, 2011, pp. 29–52.
95 G. Borgström, *Gränser för vår tillvaro* [*Limits to our Existence*] (Stockholm: LT, 1967) and, in English, G. Borgström, *The Hungry Planet: The Modern World at the Edge of Famine* (New York: Macmillan, 1965).
96 H. Palmstierna, *Svält, plundering, förgiftning* [*Famine, Plunder, Poisoning*] (Stockholm: Rabén & Sjögren,1967).
97 G. Myrdal: 'Economics of an Improved Environment'. Lecture delivered in connection with the United Nations Conference on the Human Environment, 8 June 1972, Stockholm. Published as a contribution in M. F. Strong (ed.), *Who Speaks for Earth?* (New York, 1973), pp. 67–108. Quotes in the following from stencil version in *Alva and Gunnar Myrdal Archives*.
98 The main thread we will follow here is how Myrdal exposed the environmental problems in general and specifically how it presented itself to the advanced industrial countries. His critiques of the Rome Report and the Mansholt Plan for the EEC and some his suggestions concerning the challenges for the centrally planned countries have seemed less topical in this context.
99 Thomas Malthus (1766–1834), a classical economist argued that population growth would put increasing pressure on agricultural production and eventually lead to downward pressures on living conditions generally.
100 The concept now most frequently used is Gross Domestic Product. They share the same flaws, the only difference being that while GNP includes the

activities abroad of domestically owned enterprises and excludes the domestic activities of enterprises owned and registered outside the national territory, GDP is summing up the totality of domestic economic activities, regardless of ownership relation.

101 G. Myrdal: 'Economics of an Improved Environment' (1972), p. 5.
102 Ibid., p. 9.
103 Ibid., p. 10.
104 Ibid., p. 9.
105 Ibid., p. 12.
106 Ibid., p. 16.
107 Ibid., p. 17.
108 Ibid., p. 22.
109 Ibid., p. 22.
110 Ibid,. p. 26.
111 Ibid., p. 27.
112 Ibid., p. 29.
113 G. Myrdal: 'De internationella organisationerna', *Svenska Dagbladet* 15 October 1957 and 'Det internationella samarbetets brister' *Svenska Dagbladet* 15 October 1957 (Translation ÖA).
114 This comment gives an interesting and very relevant understanding of the dynamics in the origins of the Cold War period.
115 Gunnar Myrdal: 'Increasing Interdependence between States but Failure of International Cooperation', *Felix Neubergh Lecture*, Göteborg 1977. Reprint in *Essential Gunnar Myrdal*, pp. 194–200.
116 The concept of 'stagflation' refers to the combination in Western Europe of economic stagnation (lowered growth rates) and increasing levels of inflation during the latter part of the 1970s.
117 From his *Felix Neubergh Lecture* in 1977, *Essential Gunnar Myrdal* (2005), p. 195.
118 *Challenge of World Poverty* (1970), p. 435.
119 *An American Dilemma* (1944), p. 1028.

3   Out of the European Dilemma?

Using Myrdal's ideas in the post-2008 landscape

As argued in the Introduction political and economic developments around the year 2008 mark the closure of a long phase of economical world development and the entry into a new political and economic landscape.

Considering the near meltdown of the central financial system in the autumn 2008 as the epicentre of the crisis, one can clearly see that its reverberations since have spread into other fields, creating crises that are economic and social as well as political in their nature.

The dynamics leading to the crash of the investment bank Lehman Brothers in September 2008 and its aftermath the following year stands out even more starkly with hindsight. Lehman Brothers was not a minor player, it was at the time the fourth largest investment bank in the US and trading in all major financial centres in the world. Despite very extensive assets – estimated at US\$639 billion in its petition at bankruptcy – it was heavily dependent on day-to-day financing and when it announced a quarterly loss of US\$2.8 billion due to losses in the housing market, confidence among its creditors evaporated, credits dried up and stock market values plummeted.[1] All attempts to save the bank by takeover failed, since no one could know how much of its assets were in fact 'toxic'. The bank's closure resulted in a shock wave which reverberated through the whole international banking system: with a daily turnover of several billion US dollars, the banking system is heavily dependent on liquidities to function. And willingness to borrow is in turn dependent on confidence, on the trust that the borrower will be able to service the debts. No one could know who would take the blow of the losses on the claims on Lehman Brothers, no one could know which bank was about to fail because of fictive, 'toxic' assets, and which bank wasn't. US Treasury Secretary at that time, Henry Paulson, gave a famous illustration of the situation: it was like being offered ten bottles of water, knowing that one was poisonous but not which one. Who would drink? The immediate consequence of this general loss of confidence was a drastic credit squeeze, further threatening banking institutions as well as major industrial companies, especially of the car industry. Stock markets fell more than 30 per cent world-wide in three months, industrial production in OECD countries fell by 15 per cent in the first eight months after the crash and unemployment rose by 60 per cent, putting 21 million people out of work. The overall GDP of the OECD countries fell 3.4 per cent between 2008 and 2009.[2] And these percentages are averages, realities in the economies that were hardest hit were considerably worse.

The financial crisis unleashed by the bankruptcy of Lehman Brothers was not the first one: the preceding decade had seen the Asian crisis in 1997, the currency crises in Russia 1998, Brazil 1999 and Argentina in 2001, to list some of the most conspicuous. But the financial crisis of 2008 was unparalleled in its dimensions, far exceeding the previous ones. It had a global dimension – evidenced by the development of world trade: after a drastic slowdown in the second half of 2008 world trade fell a further 11.9 per cent in 2009, for the OECD countries even 13.6 per cent. This was a slowdown unique in the whole post-war period.[3]

The dimensions of the crisis unleashed by the crash in 2008 are comparable only to that of the Wall Street Crash in 1929. In the US the effects were considerably worse after 1929: in the ensuing three years stock markets fell by 70 per cent and unemployment rose to a quarter of the 50 million strong labour force.[4] Unemployment in EU now still stands below 13 per cent on average. The overall effect of the 2008 crash on the employment level in the European Union has not been as drastic as that: its general unemployment has risen from 7.1 per cent in 2008 to 11.0 per cent in July 2013. It is mainly in the countries of southern Europe that unemployment have risen to depression levels: Spain 25 per cent, Greece 27 per cent. But the overall figures might however be misleading. In actual numbers the 29 million actually unemployed in the EU vastly outnumbers the army of unemployed in the US Depression years.

Moreover, the post-2008 years have opened two deep divides with the EU: a geographical and a generational one. While all the major northern countries in the EU still have unemployment levels below 8 per cent (Germany only 5.2 per cent) the rest of the euro area are stuck with untenable unemployment levels, well above 10 per cent. Perhaps the starkest example of EU's failure to handle the actual crisis process is the growth of youth unemployment: roughly a fourth of the labour force under 25 is unemployed. In some countries more than half of them are barred from access to work and economic independence.

It might be exaggerated to talk of the post-2008 developments as a global crisis, but in view of the much more integrated character of the world economy the ripple effects of the crisis have been significant, not only in US and some countries in Western Europe, but on all continents.[5] And in view of the much larger relative size of the financial system the losses caused by the banks have been staggering. The losses in output and volume of the major industrial economies due to the 2008 crisis have been calculated in different ways. In 2009 the Head of the Financial Direction of Bank of England Andrew G. Haldane estimated the 'systemic cost' of the bank-too-big-to-fail by calculating the loss of output between projected and actual GDP growth in 2009, which amounted to a loss of US$4 trillion, or roughly 6 per cent of world GDP. Moreover, depending on the degree to which this slowdown will be persistent, the losses in the longer run would range between US$60 and 200 trillion. These calculations are admittedly hypothetical but nevertheless reveal the dimensions of the shock waves emanating from the 2008 crash.[6] The Lehman crash in 2008 triggered a panicky reaction in the global financial system that must be likened to a stroke in an arterial system. A more profound breakdown was averted only by government interventions of a scale hitherto unseen. In an IMF-report to the G20 meeting in 2009 the total volume of the rescue and bailout operations was estimated at US$10,800 billion.[7] These rescue operations, leading to a rapid growth of government debts, are increasingly weighing upon economic development in many countries. It is therefore safe to assume that the crisis is not behind us, we are only in the midst of a crisis process. If we are to judge by the post-1929 precedent the crisis will be of a prolonged character and with occasional drastic chains of events.

A crisis of such a magnitude inevitably changes the way societies and economies operate in profound ways. The 1929 crash ushered in a protracted period of economic and social crises; it was the beginning of a series of aftershocks: notably the bankruptcy of the Austrian bank *Credit Anstalt* and Great Britain's abandonment of the Gold Standard regime in 1931. The rapid spread of mass unemployment in major industrial countries and social misery amongst the farming population, especially in the US, gave rise to a drastically changed political climate and new political regimes in the US, in Sweden and in Germany. The urge for defending separate national interests became an overwhelmingly strong concern and thereby prompted the rise of protectionist measures.

History never repeats itself, but given the depth of the financial crash and the considerably greater and deeper interdependency and integration of the major industrial countries it seems reasonable to assume that these economies – and societies – are presently caught in a crisis process that will have equally profound consequences economically, socially and politically.

At the World Economic Forum in 2009 the American-Hungarian banker Georg Soros saw recent events as the close of a post-war era characterized by credit optimism and expansion and that the era henceforth should be dominated by apprehension and growing distrust. This is of course a very broad generalization hiding an innumerable variety of situations, but is nevertheless worth reflecting on as an indication of the general climate of ideas. What is certain is, that we have henceforth a period much more dominated by insecurity than before, an insecurity that prevails on all levels: socially, politically and economically, and is felt individually as well as collectively.

In view of this the parallel with the post-1929 crisis will be pursued one step further: in the same way as that crisis period demanded and produced new paradigms in the fields of economic and social sciences we are now likewise compelled to make extensive re-evaluations of conventional knowledge and dogmas.

In such a situation: to what extent can the theoretical critique, the methodological approach and the economic and social analysis of Myrdal be a tool for such a re-evaluation? And to what extent can his methodological approach inspire us to transcend his ideas to find new solutions?

These questions will stay in focus in the concluding part of this re-assessment of Myrdal's contribution.

The dynamics of 2008 as four interlinked dynamics

The origins of the 2008 financial meltdown are in themselves a vindication of Myrdal's analysis of the basic tendency of the dynamics of the economies in industrially advanced countries: a tendency away from equilibrium, a dynamics of circular and cumulative causation links.

Why did Lehman Brothers run into such heavy losses in the first place? Primarily it was because of massive defaults in the so-called 'sub-prime'-sector of the US housing market, or put more simply: the banks had been lending massively and on false premises to poorer sections of the US population who were hoping to become owners of decent homes for the first time in their lives. These dreams were instantly crushed when the US Federal Reserve drastically raised interest rates to 'cool down' a housing market they judged as overheated. The immediate result was that about 40 per cent of loans were in default, which sent shockwaves through mortgage market institutions which finally hit investment banks like Lehman Brothers. One could discern four different cumulative processes converging to create the turmoil of 2008–2009.

The first was the long period of rising inequalities in the US (and beyond): While the top quintile of US households saw real revenues rise steadily over the previous two decades, the lower half of the US population had stagnating or decreasing real incomes. The result of this had been a steadily growing indebtedness of US households, both on mortgages and consumer credit. This increased indebtedness had first been among those who could support debt servicing, even use the loans to their own advantage with rising equity values, but with extremely low interest rates and the aggressive lending policies of financial institutions the increased indebtedness spread to a level where people were much more vulnerable to outside shocks. So, this first process was an outcome of long-term changes in the domestic distribution of wealth in the US towards deepening inequality.

The second process emerged from the breakdown of the *Bretton Woods* monetary system of semi-fixed currency relations in 1970.[8] From this time the rates of the major trading currencies fluctuated. Since the volume of international trade had increased drastically under the previous era, this meant an increased level of uncertainty for all transnational corporations. To protect themselves against this insecurity a system of 'currency insurances' – financial instruments called currency derivatives – were greatly expanded in volume and sophistication. In view of the rising importance of transnational investments 'assurances' on future interest developments became a major component of these financial instruments, the volume of which grew from 588 in 1986 to US$12,207 billion in 1997. But the other side of the 'insurance' coin is speculation. The character of this trade is extremely short-term in orientation: in 2002 the Bank for International Settlements, the intergovernmental bank keeping public statistics on these matters, estimated the four out of five international transactions had a time span shorter than a week. In such a situation the 'speculation'-character of the instruments is evidently dominating, and the volume of these transactions is dwarfing those of international trade proper, in goods and services. According to the latest account of BIS in 2008 these financial transactions represented 98 per cent of the gross volume of international transactions. This process, arriving out of a change in the relative industrial strengths of US, Germany and Japan and the inability of the US to stand by its obligation to exchange dollars to gold at a fixed rate, thus fundamentally changed the characteristics of international economic exchange – with an extremely powerful contagion effect as a result.

As a third process the technological changes in computing sciences and the Internet can be discerned and the possibilities these changes implied for innovations in the financial sector. The use of derivatives and options as means to finance business operations in all types of economic activities: industrial investments, business mergers, housing markets, insurance businesses or rescheduling public debts on all levels. The last 20 years have seen an exponential growth of new kinds of financial instruments, derivatives betting on anything: interest rates, prices of primary products, guesses on future growth patterns and so on.

What is common to them all is that they are aimed at cashing in immediately on guesses about future developments. Basically it is a zero-sum game as is any betting system, but while some are cashing in their day-to-day transactions it is left open as to who it is that will take the losses.

Moreover, to an increasing degree the transactions were concluded outside the mediation of the regulated stock market, 'over-the-counter', that is directly between traders in the major banks. The growth of these financial instruments has indeed been huge: the estimated gross volume of all these contracts – the 'outstanding notional amount' of financial derivatives – amounted to US$574 trillion in the 2010 *Triennal Survey* of the BIS.[9] To give a sense of proportion this sum equals roughly ten years of the World GDP. This unchecked growth of the financial sector betting on the future is a further element which explains the gravity of the crisis process that was triggered in 2008.

A fourth element is the deepened interconnectedness of the international banking system. In order to optimize the volume of their business banks have increasingly had recourse to inter-bank lending on a day-to-day basis. The borrower gets a loan on the fixed interbank rate betting on a higher return on its own operation, while the lender avoids having any lending capacities idle. This was seen as a perfection of the financial markets, in a way that permitted an expansion of the overall volume of the financial activities of the banks concerned. It also played an important role in the rate of returns: in 2008 the US Federal Reserve estimated that approximately 40 per cent of the overall profits of the major banks arose out of this inter-bank lending. Although profitable in good times this extreme dependency on short-time financing also made the spread effect catastrophic when one major bank failed.

In all these instances what we see are cumulative processes rapidly developing, and where constraining counter-forces have been too weak or non-existent, these interlocked dynamics have all proven to be much stronger than any of the conventional economic theories predicted. In the hearings in the US Congress on the origins of the financial crisis, former Head of the Federal Reserve Alan Greenspan admitted being taken by surprise, and said: 'It's a once in a century event.' All the elaborate econometrical methods to discern patterns of business cycles used by the economists at the IMF or at the different national authorities dealing with economic projections, fundamentally failed to predict the drastic downturn and the extent of the extreme disruption of financial markets in the autumn of 2008. In view of this fact alone the relevance of Myrdal's dynamic understanding of the basic instability of market patterns is obvious.

This understanding of the cumulative and circular causation of the factors leading to the financial crisis does not preclude another, more structural interpretation of the significance of the watershed being passed. The major focus of Myrdal's analysis is on distributional and trade issues, on how to meet challenges in creating welfare societies – and ultimately a welfare world.

However, he rarely enters the workshop and discusses the politics of production and the relation between capital and labour. Those who do, such as the economists of the regulation school, argue that the deeper roots of the financial crisis are to be found in the neo-liberal paradigm and its orientation on raising margins of profit by flexibilization of labour and globalization. They see this as a way of securing a stronger power advantage for capital in relation to labour and national governments. But such an interpretation obviously calls for more structural reforms than those proposed by Myrdal in his moral call to challenge world poverty – reforms that would necessarily address power structures in 'developed' countries.

To avoid any exaggerated structural understanding of the present watershed it must be noted that the present crisis is neither total nor global. Even if all continents were affected by the first acute phases of the crisis in 2008–2009, countries in Asia, South America and Africa were much less involved. In fact in these areas many countries are experiencing quite different economic and political circumstances than industrially advanced countries in North America, Western Europe and Japan, the so-called G3-group. Most notably countries in East and South Asia (China, India, Malaysia, South Korea) are witnessing rapid development, certainly with daunting challenges, but of a different character to those confronting the US and the countries of the European Union.

Even the challenges confronting the US and the countries of the European Union are vastly different. The similarity lies in the fact that the neoliberal paradigm has dominated development patterns on both sides of the Atlantic: economies increasingly structured by financial sector concerns, privatization pressures various sector of the public sector and welfare arrangements and increasing social inequalities. However differences also stand out: using the position of the US Dollar as the world's major trading currency, the road taken by the US administration has been to rescue the vulnerable banking system. Especially the banks that are 'too-big-to-fail' – and to postpone any return to overall fiscal and financial balances by maintaining extremely low and creating new liquidities massively via so – called 'Quantitative Easing'. Due to the very different political structure of the European Union the dilemmas of rising indebtedness are presenting themselves in a much more acute manner. In using Myrdal's ideas as a tool for reflection on ways out of the financial, economic and social crisis process triggered by the events in 2008 the chosen focus here is on how dilemmas present themselves to the countries of the European Union.

In fact, in spite of having many strong points – a globally highly skilled workforce, comparatively well developed welfare protection systems, a large economically integrated area in trade balance globally – the EU was especially hard hit by the financial aftermath of the downturn in 2008. Like other major industrial countries European governments intervened massively to rescue vulnerable banks and protect industries threatened by bankruptcies: some US$3,400 billion were spent in the first post-crisis year according to the IMF-report in 2009. Add to this the fiscal losses due to the downturn of the economies and it was evident that public deficits and public indebtedness was soaring in subsequent years. But there was a major difference between the US and the UK economies on the one hand, and the EU members on the other, especially those having the euro as a currency. The European Union had a framework prohibiting deficits over 3 per cent of GDP and indebtedness surpassing 60 per cent of GDP, and countries within the euro area had no access to easy money creation as had the US and the UK.

This constitutional constraint, which is totally irrational and was created in a quite different situation – at the beginning of the 1990s – forces EU member states to apply austerity measures, cutting down on welfare and public employment to reduce public deficits – thus further aggravating the recession tendencies, especially in economically weaker countries. From 2010 the European political scene has been dominated by recurrent crises in the public finances of EU countries especially those in southern Europe (Portugal, Greece, Spain and Italy), but also countries in Eastern Europe (Estonia, Latvia, Hungary), and Ireland has been severely hit. The response in Europe to the failure of the neo-liberal economic paradigm has thus been – an even sharper application of neo-liberal ideas on how to cure public finance. The massive costs of the operation to save the banking system from the effects of their reckless speculation has thus to be carried by their populations who in the first place are not responsible for what has gone wrong. The glaring injustice of this orientation, and the irrationality of economic policies dictated by the politico-economic establishment in the European Commission and the European Central Bank are encountering growing popular opposition in several countries and national tensions are increasing. The dilemma between balanced public finances and social justice seems intractable.

Five years after the triggering shock of the financial crash in the autumn of 2008 the continuing aftershocks have thus developed into a crisis in the European Union that is not only economic but social and political as well. The massive rise in regional disparities and youth unemployment and the glaring inadequacies of the EU as an institution has created a popular rejection that is threatening the whole edifice of the Union.

The ecological crisis: the inexorable growth of the pressure on the ecological balance

The interlinked crisis process triggered by the financial crash in 2008 was for several reasons not completely global in its reach: as noted above, some areas of the world (in Asia, South America and Africa) have experienced a different kind of social and economic dynamic compared with the experience of North America, Europe and Japan.

Another crisis which is, however, truly global in its consequences is the ecological crisis. Gunnar Myrdal's pessimistic forebodings of 1972 have largely been realised. Even if some of the pesticides causing the outcry in the 1960's have been prohibited, pollution has become a more generalized problem with the pervasive use of new chemical techniques in all types of production. Even when regulatory mechanisms have been established the combined effects of all the new chemical ingredients introduced is extremely hard to evaluate. The depletion of non-renewable resources has gained a renewed urgency with the rapid economic development of the Asian giants. Even when limits have proven less definite than predicted – the peak of oil production has been postponed several times – the technical challenges involved in tapping into resources ever more difficult to access is greatly increasing the environmental risks involved. A number of ecological catastrophes such as the blow-out of the oil fields in the Mexican Gulf in 2009 and the nuclear disaster in Fukushima, Japan in 2011 have shown the inadequacy of present political institutions – and indeed of markets – in handling such risks.

Certainly – a lot of progress has been made when it comes to measurement of the ecological impact of human activity, even down to detailing the 'ecological footprint' of specific products purchased by the consumer. Considerable technological advances have also been accomplished in production, for instance making cars less polluting and energy consuming.

But the main failures on a systemic level persist – and are aggravated. There is still no relevant ecological balance in the transportation system between road, rail, water and air. The predominance of transport by road – heavily supported by the car industry – is vastly greater than when Myrdal signalled the problem in 1972 and is now spreading to countries like China and India. As regards long distance transport, energy consuming airborne transport is supplanting maritime methods that are much more sensible from an ecological point of view. The absurdity of food chains, evoked by Georg Borgström – referred to by Myrdal in his lecture in 1972 – has now deepened and the situation is definitely aggravated. Agricultural giants in a handful of countries (US, France, Argentine, Brazil, Australia, Thailand

and a few others) are out-competing local agriculture in several underdeveloped countries, thereby further contributing to global social imbalances. Even foodstuffs harvested and consumed locally in developed countries (fishery products for example) are now inserted in 'globalized' food chains, 'outsourcing' parts of the production and packaging to distant low-wage countries, making them latter-day globetrotters. As for energy systems they are still predominantly geared towards extraction models–instead of economizing – how to get more rather than how to use less. On this point rapid economic development in China has added a new local instance of grave ecological concern.

In general, the dilemma between the immediate search for individual gain and the long term effects on the fragile biological balance of the earth has become ever more acute. Despite multiple warnings the rainforests are diminishing, desertification continues and biodiversity is severely strained in many areas. In addition to these developments the overarching problem of climate change has become urgent. As scientists have shown, the combined effects of industrialization and urbanization, the accelerated use of fossil energy in production, transports and heating have increased the emission of carbon-dioxide in such a way that results in a gradual but inexorable rise of temperature levels. A development that in itself is triggering a number of climate changes: the melting of polar ices and glaciers leading to changes of ocean currents and raising sea levels with predictable inundation of densely populated areas and island nations as a consequence. Other predicted consequences of climate change are increased volatility of climate, and increased frequency of extreme weather conditions and subsequent 'natural' catastrophes.

Myrdal suggested that the impulse for a profound reconsideration of the conditions – and the limits – for economic growth should come not from economists but from experts in the natural sciences. On that point he has really been vindicated. The largely increased public awareness of the ecological dangers confronting us is primarily due to the thousands of devoted researchers in geology, climatology, chemistry and other natural sciences – and those who have popularized their findings. In particular, since 1988 our awareness of the dangers inherent in climate change has acquired a valuable new institutional mechanism as reference point: the Intergovernmental Panel on Climate Change (IPCC). The Panel was set up by the World Meteorological Organisation (WMO) and the United Nations Environment Program (UNEP) after a decision by the UN General Assembly in 1988. Its recurrent Assessment Reports, produced by the cooperation of more than 800 researchers, are synthesizing all actual knowledge on climate change and are studying longer historical sequences and evaluate their combinatory effects.[10] Certainly there are still sceptics. Some voices have even questioned the whole idea of human-induced climate changes, arguing the inevitable uncertainty of long term prognoses. Fortunately, the vast statistical work that has been accomplished and the trans-disciplinary considerations of the role of interactions have made it possible to reduce uncertainties and to present conclusions that are supported by an overwhelming majority of the scientists involved. The main gist of their conclusions is that if current trends are not arrested within the coming 20 to 30 years the climate change will be irreversible and of dimensions that are even more difficult to calculate.

What is hopeful in this situation is that the awareness of the general public has greatly increased alongside with scientific knowledge. There have also been some positive intergovernmental agreements reached that tackle the issue of climate change. The agreement on Clear Development Mechanism ratified in 2005, the so-called 'Kyoto Protocol' signed by 37 OECD countries, was a binding agreement on clearly defined targets in changing the trends of carbon dioxide emission.[11] A significant flaw in this agreement was however, that the country that had worst record on this account – the United States – refused to be bound by any international agreement that was not of its own making. When the Kyoto Protocol expired there were great expectations that it would be extended and accepted more universally at the UN Conference on Environment in Copenhagen in 2009. It was the largest UN Conference ever organized outside New York, with 115 heads of state present and some 40,000 representatives from governments and non-governmental organizations of all kinds from all parts of the world. What happened instead was that the Kyoto agreement with its binding targets was abandoned and replaced by general and non-committing statements. Even if a total breakdown was avoided in the final hours, the Copenhagen Accord finally accepted fell short of all expectations. The fundamental reason for this was differences on distributional issues. Who should make the greatest efforts – those who polluted most or those whose emissions increased most, due to their economic growth? On this issue the developing countries insisted on putting the burden on the OECD countries whose emissions per capita were several times higher than those of the rest of the world. The industrial countries on the other hand, and especially the United States, wanted binding promises from China, whose massive use of coal in industrial development greatly increased China's share of the emission of greenhouse gases. Bolivia's president Evo Morales also raised the historical dimension of the problem and the question of the 'ecological debt'. After all, it was the industrial development in Europe, North America and Japan that had caused the ecological imbalances in the first place. These countries had an 'ecological debt' towards Mother Earth, – towards *Pachamama* in the world view of the Andean indigenous peoples. A debt these countries should assume fully before demanding sacrifices of other nations. Finally there was also the question of technology: rich, industrially developed countries had ample access to new technologies which offered less polluting processes and reductions of emissions of green house gases. On what terms would the poorer countries get access to such new technologies, wouldn't this be yet another way for rich countries to continue to dominate the poorer ones? The failure of the Copenhagen Conference showed once again that the distributional issue is a fundamental aspect of the ecological crisis, an issue on which every concerned individual and nation must take a stand, as Myrdal so forcefully pointed out 40 years ago.

Even aside from the solution to these distribution issues it is obvious that the ecological challenges will demand profound changes in development patterns and ways of organization in every society. The climate changes that are already happening are yet another drastic illustration that the fundamental attitude of economics and economic development in relation to nature has to be changed. The 'productivism' geared at GDP-growth – even in its more benign, 'welfare' version – has to be replaced by a framework where the necessities of long term ecological balances provide the fundamental restrictions within which political choices can operate. In that sense the continued central role of GDP as an aggregate measure as to the state of an economy is totally misleading. Not only are they – as Myrdal pointed out – based on partial, arbitrary and biased measurements, they are also leading away from ecological concerns. A major effort in the countries with high green-house emissions must be oriented towards economizing, consuming less by changing modes of production, transportation and consumption. Such changes would appear as decreases in GDP but would in fact be an increase in quality in terms of societal organization.

The socio-political crisis process in Europe triggered by the financial crisis in 2008 and the ecological crisis of climate change has very different time frames. The former is a process that is a pressing urgency that will find a solution in one way or the other within a matter of five or ten years. The latter will be increasingly felt but necessary actions and choices are more easily postponed. It challenges our capacity to comprehend future dangers, not only reacting to urgent problems. In that way it is a much more demanding task. A task where Myrdal's moral approach seems all the more prescient.

Myrdal's approach as a tool in this new landscape

Given this picture of the crisis confronting us: how can Myrdal's ideas and general approach be a useful tool? This section will provide an indication of a number of points where his ideas are particularly relevant.

His theoretical critique of conventional neo-classic economics

The massive failure of neo-liberal economics is just as profound as was that of the neo-classical economists Myrdal criticized in the 1930s. As Paul Krugman wrote at the outbreak of the crisis:

> Few economists saw our current crisis coming, but this predictive failure was the least of the field's problems. More important was the profession's blindness to the very possibility of catastrophic failures in a market economy.... The economics profession went astray because economists as a group, mistook beauty, clad in impressive-looking mathematics, for truths ... economists fall back in love with the old.[12]

The econometric exercises on the basis of abstract and unrealistic models must be challenged by altogether new approaches in political economy. Myrdal's call for a 'new economy' has been one of many and is actually pursued in many different quarters. There are a variety of schools pursuing this critique: post-Keynesians, ecological economists and regulationist economists. But so far they have had difficulty in establishing themselves in the general debate. There is a lesson on the organizational level to be drawn from the continuing dominance of neo-liberal economics in university education: the heterodox currents need to establish firm institutional bases to be heard.

Criticizing the concept of Gross Domestic Product

Although initially being a very 'pro-growth' economist, Myrdal was equally early in presenting a stringent critique of the concept. The necessity of dethroning it as guiding tool for macro-economics has become urgent. The report of the economic commission headed by Joseph Stiglitz, Amartya Sen and Jean-Paul Fitoussi in 2010[13] went a long way in presenting new criteria for a broader concept of growth. It is appalling to note that in a political climate dominated by demands for austerity measures, international institutions and national governments are still far away from giving these due consideration, rather going in the opposite direction. Could it be the task of a new, independently funded research institute?

The trans-disciplinary approach

One of the reasons why conventional economics has succeeded in remaining immune to criticism is its sectarianism, its insistence on economics as a science proper. Its approaches of abstract modelling, such as 'rational choice' assumptions, have even been exported to social and psychological sciences. Heterodox economists should follow Myrdal's example and go the opposite way, embracing a trans-disciplinary approach. No 'new economy' – however theoretically brilliant – can provide necessary answers unless it is immersed in the social and political realities of the problem. Any economy is at heart social, it is dealing with human relations, attitudes and institutions.

The insistence on the inescapability of values

Myrdal continually emphasized that values are guiding our research, whether we admit it or not. Furthermore values accompany us continually in research proper. Simply put – there can be no answer unless a question is asked. There can be no view without a viewpoint. A prime duty of the scientist is to reflect on values and try to present them as transparently as possible. When economists hide their values behind 'objectivist' pretentions and declarations of 'necessities' there can be no rational debate, even less a democratic one. On the other hand, when conflicting values are openly presented it is possible both to evaluate the relevance of the questions and the validity of the results. Since the crisis now confronting us – especially in Europe – is at heart a social crisis – it is the social realities of larger sections of the populations that must be the starting points for questions asked.

The pertinence of the core values of Myrdal: rationality, equality and democracy

Myrdal is properly to be seen as part of the current of radical liberalism in the US born out of the experiences of economic depression and the war against fascism. He constantly referred to the ideals of Enlightenment, to rationalism and egalitarian and democratic values as guiding principles. In the new political landscape these core values seem to be quite relevant starting points when trying to address the current challenges.

Full employment as a moral issue

When preparing the post-war programme of the Swedish labour movement Myrdal advanced the idea of an 'economy at full steam' as a motto. It was invoking the irrationality of leaving human and material capacities of creating welfare idle, regarding it as an irresponsible waste of resources. This was formulated as a sharp critique of the economic theories that were accepting mass unemployment as a natural consequence of the unwillingness of workers to adapt to market conditions by lowering their wages.

Full employment was therefore in Myrdal's view not a consequence of a successful economic policy but an organizing idea. Full employment had to be planned, not only wished for. This idea has to be re-affirmed again and developed with an ever greater insistency. This has become urgent after decades during which structural mass unemployment has become accepted as a measure of disciplining social resistance of the trade unions against ongoing deterioration of rights and livelihood. In a situation where the general level of officially registered unemployment in the European Union is well over 10 per cent, and where in some countries more than 50 per cent of its youth is denied access to work, there can be no more pressing issue than to reaffirm the value of full employment. These levels of unemployment are not only a question of irrationality in leaving useful forces idle, still more important are the profoundly destructive effects that prolonged periods of unemployment have – both individually and socially. Being unemployed is not a static condition, it is being caught in a destructive process: a process of social marginalization, a gradual sapping of individual self-esteem and competence – often reinforced by humiliating experiences at workfare centres and unsuccessful job applications. Unemployment is equally disrupting socially as it disenfranchises large sections of the population. The gulf between outside and inside conditions of employment security is everywhere present and works as a force disciplining everyone, forcing people to submit to the power of autocratic structures in all workplaces, undermining any belief in equal rights and democracy. Mass unemployment is destroying the very links that create society. Work is a fundamentally social activity. Having a remunerated activity is giving the individual both a relative autonomy and a social context. The fundamentally social role of employment should therefore be emphasized in societies so easily torn by ethnic, communitarian, nationalistic or generational divides. The fundamental flaw of the recurrent demand for 'basic citizen salaries' as a solution to unemployment is that it doesn't recognize this social role.

How the right – and duty – to work should be organized is however another question. A question dealing with how to share the fruits of collectively created resources and welfare. Which choice should be made between individual autonomy and social inclusion? Ideas are in abundance in this domain. It would seem reasonable that general reduction of hours in work-days/work-weeks and of work-sharing schemes which include the unemployed would increase the individual autonomy of those employed, and at the same time reduce the misery of unemployment. Similarly the question of the transfer of professional knowledge between generations is a large field yet to be adequately explored. It is equally absurd that elderly people are constrained to work on to secure reasonable pensions and thus bar young people from access to employment, as is the pressure by employers in forcing active and qualified labour to early retirement only to recruit cheaper and more amenable young people. The role of practical experience in acquiring professional knowledge is vastly underestimated in our societies. Work schemes with elderly and young people working side by side in transition periods would serve both to alleviate burdens of the pre-retirement years and secure a broader transfer of knowledge to future generations. Still another choice to be made is that of life-long learning and the possibility of alternating orientations of work. The possibilities of alternating periods of employment with periods of study or sabbaticals would also fit within the general framework of the right and duty of everyone to work in a society in constant transition.

Full employment must again become the most important obligation for society, anything less would be a fatal capitulation in efforts to create inclusive societies.

Welfare society and modernity

Linked to Myrdal's call for full employment was that of a welfare society. Alva and Gunnar Myrdal were among the most prominent social reformers in Sweden and their ideas for vast social reforms in the post-war years were largely inspired by British liberal William Beveridge's call for 'freedom from need' that was the basis of the post-war reforms for decent housing, basic retirement pensions and child allowances for young families. This was also the reason for their demands for a large expansion of education – proposed and enacted. Ignorance should be reduced through education. Organization of child care was also a question of affirming the equal rights of women to employment and citizenship. Ultimately Gunnar and Alva Myrdal regarded the welfare society as a question of modernity.

The first post-war decades reaffirmed this modernity in Europe. The social safety nets expanded on almost all fronts: it was no longer an economic calamity to be sick, unemployed or old. Even poor people could afford to study and the public sector offered many people employment in health, social services, and education. This meant developing and maintaining society infrastructure at large. In general the welfare societies that developed in post-war Europe can be regarded as ways of organizing the unity of production and reproduction, necessary in any society.

This modernity has however been undermined and under constant attack from neo-liberal forces during the last 20 years. These forces are intent on turning societies into markets. The functioning of the industrial production site and of private enterprise has been taken as an ideal model and adapted to various sectors. This approach is part and parcel of the tendency of neo-liberal economic theorists to colonize other sciences and fields of knowledge: market models used by economists are considered as superior knowledge to those of the professionals working in health services, education, childcare and so on. Present accounting systems are geared accordingly: the work of the employed appears solely as costs and not as assets and the development of the quality of their work is assumed as a zero productivity growth.

These attacks have caused major dysfunctions within the public sectors of economies and have paved the way for the plundering of taxpayer funded activities by private enterprise. But the basic organizations of the welfare societies are not beyond repair. It is urgent to reaffirm the modernity of the welfare society and to reconstruct and develop this modernity by building on the professional knowledge of the employed in dialogue with citizens-users. The trade-off assumed by neo-liberals between freedom and protection is false: safety nets are not inducing passivity, and the lack of them produces not freedom but fear. Where people have confidence in safety nets they can dare to try new ventures. This is the optimistic message inherent in the promises of a welfare society and it is still relevant.

Disciplining capital: High taxes and low interest rates

When Myrdal developed his ideas of creating a welfare society there was a relative balance of forces between capital and labour in Sweden. This was also the case with the welfare projects in the UK, France and other European countries. Myrdal was aware of the need to harness business interests for immediate profits, and to orient its dynamics in line with concerns of long term development. We have noted how he wanted to favour the 'modern industrialist' and curb the *rentier* by a fiscal policy of 'High taxes, low interest rates'. The idea was that all endeavours at long term investments would be favoured by cheap lending conditions and tax deductions, but all dividends for shareholders should be heavily taxed. At present, economic policies have been oriented rather the opposite way. They have permitted collusion between executives and major shareholders to plunder the assets of major industrial concerns and private banks. Corporate executives have been focusing on 'shareholder value' and high dividends as the main objective using different techniques in rigging the share values upward. And shareholders have abetted the executives by pegging their remunerations to these increases.[14] Governments have been aggravating this pattern by competing to attract or retain businesses by lowering taxes on capital and increasing a myriad of tax exemptions – to such a degree that the general rate of net taxation of capital has been heavily reduced. These concessions to business interests have not produced expected results in increases in investment. Layoffs and downsizing – while still paying out considerable dividends – have on the contrary been a recurrent strategy for major shareholders to secure high share values. In such a situation, where the short-termism of shareholders is dominant, it is obvious that a new – or old – approach of disciplining capital is needed to secure investments for industries and banks in general. Industries and banks have social responsibilities towards the societies in which they have been able to prosper, and towards the working forces whose labour has produced the wealth they are representing. Any freedom demanded by business interests must be reciprocated by responsibility. A clearly assumed return to higher taxation on capital is a question of social justice and responsibility.

Transcending Myrdal: debt, credits and new growth paradigms

These overall principles may have a broad appeal but don't they lack realism in the world of today? How could countries with high public debts afford large efforts to combat unemployment? And wouldn't the only result of raising taxation on enterprises be a further flight abroad? This is precisely the kind of question that is forcing us to go beyond the ideas of Gunnar Myrdal.

This necessity is of course basically due to the fact that the present situation is so radically different to the world of the 1940s – and even the 1970s – when Myrdal developed his ideas. Differences due both to the process of integration of the international economy – its 'globalization' to use a buzz word – and the effects of the crisis process triggered in 2008.

In going beyond some of Myrdal's ideas on economy one may still be inspired by his approach to transcending dilemmas. We will deal with the problems of the social responsibility of private enterprise, the question of debts, credits and public accounts.

Tax evasion as social irresponsibility

A significant feature of the preceding decades of 'globalization' has been the staggering use of tax havens as a means for financial institutions, transnational companies and rich individuals to escape the duty of paying the taxes. These are taxes that have been democratically decided in their resident countries, or in the areas of their main activities. This is seen by the concerned parties as a technical procedure: the term used is 'fiscal optimisation'. A recent report by the research organization *Global Finance Integrity*[15] estimated that the illicit financial yearly flows out of developing countries amounted to between US$856 and 1,060 billion yearly.[16] Bearing in mind the integrated character of the world economy, where at least half of the international trade is taking place within the multinationals, it is evident that the amount of tax evasion practiced by banks and multinationals active in the European Union would add significantly to that volume of illicit activities. Furthermore, wealth is stashed away in those 'tax havens'. In another report by the same author it was estimated that the total assets so-called *High Net Wealth Individuals (HNWIs)* in tax havens amounted to approximately US$21 trillion in 2010.[17]

Euphemistically these practices are called 'fiscal optimization' by the financial institutions involved. Tax evasion would however be a more correct denomination. The consequent loss of tax revenue for developing countries amounts to between US$98 and 106 billion, 4 per cent of the world's total tax revenues. The loss of revenue for developed countries is probably of the same magnitude.

These practices have been actively condoned by governments in all the major industrial countries. They have even sometimes organized their own pet tax haven. In the United States the state of Delaware serves as such an outlet for 'tax-shy' businesses, and in Great Britain the City of London enjoys an extra-territoriality considerably lowering taxation.

In addition to the considerable losses of tax revenues incurred, the tax havens also function as veritable green-houses for international criminality, their strict codes of bank secrecy permit money laundering on a massive scale.

These practices nevertheless have enjoyed widespread support. Banks and business interests have found an easy way of earning more money, rich individuals putting their savings in far away funds in Luxemburg, Cayman Islands or Singapore are pleased to find an extra 10 or 15 per cent yearly return with no taxes to be paid.

Fundamentally the whole system of tax havens is an immoral aberration. After all taxes are a civic duty, a recognition of each individual's social responsibility to the society of which he or she is a part. Financial institutions and businesses should pay taxes in the country where their major activities are developed, since they are relying on its institutions to function and prosper. Tax evasion of any kind is from a moral point of view, an act of social irresponsibility even when legal formalities are used as fig leaves. The permissiveness of governments in condoning the development of these practices is a passivity that makes them accessory to criminal activities.

The costs incurred by public economies in the last five years of financial and economic crisis have been a stark revelation of the fundamental iniquities of tax haven activities, and governments in search of revenues have begun to talk of regulations that could limit tax evasion and harmonize taxation levels. This need is also recognized in the general declarations against tax evasion of the G20 group in 2009. But now there is an urgent need to go beyond declarations, and to undertake affirmative action. Some steps have already been taken, but as the scrutiny by *Tax Justice Network*[18] shows, most of the measures remain to be taken. Effectively curtailing tax havens, morally delegitimizing any bank, business or individual using them, is a prerequisite for fiscal policies that strive to be socially just.

Debt – whose debts?

When Myrdal discussed ways of servicing the public debt, heavily increased by the war years, without cutting down on social expenditures, he was a pioneer in showing the dynamic effects of economic growth as a way out of that dilemma. In the present situation this will not suffice. In the major industrial countries there has been a long-term tendency towards an increase in public indebtedness. This is due to a combination of factors: slow growth, unrewarded public generosity towards business interests and tax evasion. With the onslaught of the financial crisis in 2008 the scale of this process changed drastically. Now public indebtedness is predicted to rise dramatically in all major industrial countries in the coming years. The threat of a debt crisis for these countries comparable to the one endured by developing countries in the 1980s and 1990s has been invoked, and is only allayed by the exceptionally low interest rates offered in most countries. Past experiences of debt-ridden developing countries are not promising: they had to endure a lost decade with hard 'structural adjustment programmes' to receive just enough money from the IMF and other institutions to pay interest on their debt but nothing more. Even if the public debt problems in Japan, Great Britain and the United States seem to be more intractable in the long term, it is in the European Union that the question of the public indebtedness is raised most pressingly.

The reason for this is purely institutional. The EU Treaty establishes fixed norms on indebtedness and budget deficits of the individual countries, forbids the European Central Bank from lending direct support to governments in need, the way other central banks do, and forces its member countries to turn to financial markets to finance public debts. Markets regulated by private credit rating agencies. This is a vicious system rewarding the financially strong countries with low interest rates and punishing the weak ones with interest rates that are impossible to service.

This is a vicious and arbitrary system, forcing bleeding countries to austerity measures, increasing unemployment and poverty. Real wage levels in Greece have gone down 30 per cent in the four years of five austerity programmes and there is no improvement in sight. The European Union as a whole is caught in an infernal process, creating havoc among its populations. This process is threatening the whole fabric of the Union. To escape from this vicious – indeed infernal – circle some fundamental questions must be asked concerning debts. Who is vulnerable? Which debts are legitimate?

Who is vulnerable? The first thing to notice is the fundamentally flawed measure of public indebtedness used by the EU treaty. It is a measuring of the gross indebtedness while not taking into account the financial assets of the public sector. Normally when assessing financial situations both assets and liabilities are taken into account. When this is done, the dimensions of public debts invariably appear less threatening. Taking France as an example: when financial assets are taken into account, its public indebtedness diminishes from 75 per cent of GDP to 40 per cent.[19] Indebtedness is thus used as a moral scarecrow – as a debt rolled over to future generations. The implication being that the lower the public debt the more moral the generational transfer. But this is a fundamentally biased notion, obscuring the fact that what is transferred is not only debt – but a society of knowledge and infrastructures. What if all investments in future projects were cancelled to diminish public indebtedness? Would our children thank us on receiving ruins to re-establish? The current understanding of public debt is biased – and it is a neo-liberal bias: the lesser the part of public investment in the economy the better. This bias is also evident when applying the gross notion of indebtedness to financial institutions. Following the same official French statistics we find that the gross indebtedness of financial institutions was five times greater than that of the French public sector, almost four times the national GDP. The pattern is the same for other EU countries with a reputation of stability such as Germany and Sweden. Of course the French banks also had financial assets roughly equal to their liabilities but as the financial crash in 2008 showed, such assets are much more volatile than the public assets in social security systems. The question of vulnerability is of vital importance in the economic systems: the greater the risk the higher the interest rate to be paid. By systematically over-estimating the vulnerability of governments and underestimating the vulnerability of the private financial system in the European Union, the current biased view on vulnerabilities gives financial institutions of all sorts an extortionist power over the weakest economies of the Union. It is always governments that have to gain the confidence of the markets, not the other way around. If the real vulnerability of the over-expanded financial actors was taken into account, a chain reaction of bankruptcies would be the logical reaction. Many economists have criticized the dysfunctions of the institutional arrangements in the European Union. To scrap the ideo-logically biased presentation of gross public debts would be a first step towards enabling a more level headed evaluation of vulnerability in the economy.

A second question to be asked is which debts are legitimate? In all resolutions of bankruptcies the question of so-called 'odious debts' has been raised. A public debt is declared odious when 'contracted by a des-potic regime for purposes alien to those of the nation and its citizens' following the standard definition given in 1927 by Alexander Sack, a professor in international law.[20] In an actualized version the Centre for International Sustainable Development at the McGill University, Toronto, Canada defines as odious debts those that are 'contracted against the interests of the citizens of a country, without their consent and with the full awareness of creditors of this state of affairs'.[21] It is for example, by no means reasonable that the actual governments of Congo-Kinshasa should service a public debt contracted under the dictatorship of Mobuto, which to a large extent was a debt feeding his personal accounts in Switzerland. Arguing along these lines the president of Ecuador, Rafael Corréa, set up an Audit Commission of internationally respected economists evaluating which parts of Ecuador's public debt was to be considered odious and which should be properly serviced. It resulted in an agreement between Ecuador and its major creditors, writing off a considerable part of those debts.[22]

These questions are increasingly asked by populations in debt-stricken countries in southern Europe. A substantial part of their public debts were contracted by the major German and French banks at profitable interest rates which the banks knew were unserviceable. These exorbitant interest rates – ranging from 7 per cent on Spanish government bonds to 12 per cent on Greek government bonds – were themselves a result of the ways the financial markets were rigged to extract profits. Huge gains were reaped by speculating on government defaults via financial instruments produced by various financial institutions, so-called Credit Default Swaps. This was an extortionist vicious circle, where default warnings from credit rating agencies, increased interest rates, increased the likelihood of defaults, increasing the value of the CDS's and the profits on weak gov-ernment bonds. This rigged financial system, characterized as a 'Pompe à phynance' by the French economist Frédéric Lordon,[23] is largely due to the refusal of the European Central Bank to support the euro area governments in the same way as central banks in the US and Great Britain.

Debts contracted under such conditions must be refused as odious. The link between public debts and popular consent is here particularly important to notice.

Credits – who is creditworthy?

A second concept that has to be re-evaluated is that of credits. It is closely linked to that of money. In its simplest form credit is the money lent by a person or institution with savings to another person or institution with projects, things to do or create. The basic function of banks is supposed to be to act as the intermediaries in this process, the savings deposits serving as a basis for lending activities.

This idea that money is a material thing is still very common. It is frequently used as an argument for cutting down on public expenditures: 'There is no money left! You can't spend what you don't have!' In reality money as a material thing represents less than 5 per cent of the world's money in circulation, and the bank lending activities are dwarfing their assets proper ten or twenty times. In real life money and credits are a flow, not a material thing, a flow where trust and time dimensions are crucial. The last thirty years of 'globalization' and 'financiarization' have witnessed an enormous hypertrophy of the financial sector that has very little to do with being an intermediate for real investments. In the global economy transactions directly linked to exchanges of products or commodities represent less than 2 per cent of the volume of international financial transactions. The rest is basically trading guesses: derivatives betting on currencies, interest rates, commodities anddefaults of one kind or another. The global volume of these transactions amounted to US$567 trillion in 2012, a figure more than six times larger than the World GDP that year.[24] The Bank for International Settlements estimated the daily trading volume of financial instruments in September 2011 to be more than US$5,000 billion.[25] It has declined somewhat since then but it is a clear reminder of the overall vulnerability of the financial system.

The primary occupation of the 'financial industry' in the last decades has been credit creation through financial innovation. This myriad of complicated instruments was of course created in order to create gain, the larger the amounts guaranteed – the larger the profits. This credit creation has ultimately been permitted by financial authorities, due to their firm belief in the efficiency of financial markets. The greater the liquidity, the more appropriate the market evaluation. It was as if markets were infallible. What the financial crisis of 2008 demonstrated however was that they were not infallible. From point of view of the financial institutions it was a winning game: 'Heads I win, tails you lose'. The knack was to jump off the guessing train in time.

The Lehman Brothers crash showed that the whole financial system was to a large extent a house of cards ultimately needing the state as saviour and lenders of last resort. Everywhere it was obvious that it was only the central banks – and the governments behind them – that were institutions worthy credit.

The era of limitless private credit creation in the form of financial instruments must come to an end. Banks must be forced to assume all the risks they take and they should not be allowed to issue assurances they can't honour.

A simple question must be asked: who is worthy of credit? When an individual enters a bank to ask for a loan, a number of questions are asked. What are your assets and liabilities? What kind of revenues do you have and how stable are they in the future? By such standards almost all the major European banks would fail the test. Even when they return to the more strict requirements (the so-called Basel II criteria) their outstanding liabilities will still be more than tenfold their capital proper, and critics have been heard to say than even this capital proper might contain assets of a volatile, perhaps even toxic nature. Moreover their projected revenues are heavily dependent on overall economic conditions over which they have a very limited influence. In comparison the credit-worthiness of the government institutions managing public debts appears in general to be much stronger. The public sector in EU countries command vast assets in infrastructure and financial resources and once action is taken against tax evasion they can count on stable revenues, if appropriate fiscal policies are applied. Even for the most debt-ridden countries debt servicing would be feasible, once interest rates are brought down to reasonable levels, and once the ECB starts working like other central banks. A lesson from the aftermath of the financial crash in 2008 must be that it is the governments, and not the private financial institutions that are worthy of credit – and credit creation.

In the present situation it must be affirmed that it is the government agencies in the European Union, individually and above all jointly, that should be the primary issuers of credits. But credits to do what? If we return to the example of the individual borrower from the bank, the wisdom of the bank issuing a credit must depend on the use of the same credit. Whether or not it is purposeful. At present central banks of Japan, US, UK and finally also the European Central Bank have resorted to massive credit creation in order to keep financial markets afloat. The method of 'Quantitative Easing' is used to flood private banks with credits at extremely low interest. The idea being that the banks will use these credits to promote investment in the private sector, thereby restarting anaemic economic growth. So far this flooding of liquidities has had very little effect on investments: with economies in recession, and great uncertainties and anxiety about future prospects, businesses delay investments and households try to reduce expenditures and debts. The liquidities put to the disposal of the banks are instead increasingly diverted to speculation on financial markets (commodity markets, government bonds and so on) and hiding the extent of their toxic assets in their balance sheets.

It is to be feared that this flooding of the financial system will end in new financial crashes, again at the expense of the public sector economies and ultimately: at the expense of the tax payers.

The actual orientation of public credit creation in the EU is misdirected, it is permitting the banks to escape responsibility for their own risk-taking, and it is destroying credit to no useful purpose. What is needed instead is a purposeful use of new financial resources. Returning to the question of full employment: what is necessary are comprehensive investment programmes which are aimed at a reconstruction of the undermined welfare societies, geared towards another kind of growth pattern, towards an ecological transition of our economies and societies. Both the general and the specific orientation of such an initiative is well developed by many European economists, notably those of the *EuroMemorandum* Group.[26]

New institutions must be created jointly to issue the financial instruments needed. The question of producing not only Euro Bonds but also Union Bonds has been raised by respected economists and politicians.[27] It is only on that level that the resources needed for long term investment programmes in various countries can be created.I Initiatives on par with – or rather larger than – the resources channelled by the 'Marshall Plan' for Western Europe in 1948 are necessary. It is an approach reminiscent of the Myrdal's and Sweden's vast credit allowances in 1944 for post-war reconstruction.

Such initiatives would undoubtedly be received with strong public approval in various European countries that so far havereceived only bad news and broken promises from the governing institutions of the European Union. This potential approval enables us to turn the questions of credit-worthiness away from the credit rating agencies and biased neo-liberal thinktanks to that of public opinion. Those initiatives that are regarded as wise, constructive and socially just are credit-worthy. There is a link between money, credits and democracy. Stability is not to be found in gold assets or formal or arbitrary criteria like those actually governing the EU. Stability is to be found in a long term project of building a welfare society and having the approval of an educated public opinion.

Deficits, financial and monetary policies – and the long run

Where does that leave us with the question of budget deficits? Let's first start with the norm of the 3 per cent level of acceptable budget deficits. This level was established arbitrarily in negotiations between the Ministers of Finance of the European Union in the beginning of the 1990s. It is now to be enforced in dramatically different circumstances, where rising deficits have been caused by external effects. That the concerted efforts in all EU countries to focus on deficit reduction would sharpen the economic recession without easing public deficits was evident to any economist versed in Keynesian economics. Myrdal's analysis of vicious economic circles in the 1930's is evidently all the more relevant today when the public sector economy carries a considerably larger weight. The question is rather: how could anyone believe that concerted austerity would not produce recession? A possible answer could be the basically biased view in some economic quarters. For convinced neo-liberals and for certain business interests the current crisis *is* the solution. In an anaemic economic situation, where common profit margins are weakened, the crisis is an extraordinary opportunity for rearranging the social fabric of societies: flexibilization of labour, fire-sales of public assets, privatizations of public services and so on – they all offer new sources of revenue.

In such a situation basic questions must be asked about public accounting systems. In the 1930s Myrdal noted the anomaly of the annual balancing requirements of public accounts in view of the pluri-annual length of business cycles. This variation is not taken into account with calculations of 'structural deficits' but how can they be calculated when even business cycles seem out of order? The speed with which public deficits in the EU are supposed to return to acceptable levels is completely arbitrary.

But more fundamentally – how are these accounts established? What is defined as running expenditures and what is regarded as investments? The difference is of importance since running expenditures are expected to be covered by yearly revenues, while investments are presumed to be amortized in the longer run and offset by its generally profitable effects. In 1945 Gunnar Myrdal raised a question in the Swedish Parliament that still has not received an answer to my knowledge: 'why are expenditures on education and research accounted as running costs? Shouldn't they to some extent be accounted as investments?' To discern to what extent these expenditures should be viewed is not an easy operation but it is very relevant. It is also – however – easy to see why his question never was answered: it would have considerably increased the margins of legitimate public intervention in the economy.

At present, the so-called 'Growth and Stability Pact' of the EU works as a neo-liberal straitjacket on public debate and on the democratic sovereignty of parliament. The public is left with biased statistics producing biased conclusions. To challenge the arbitrariness and biases of the present accounting system, must therefore also be a part of the efforts to transcend actual dilemmas.

Summing-up the relevance Myrdal's guiding ideas in addressing the European Dilemma and the need for renewal

The major strength of all post-war welfare economists – and Myrdal was one of them – was their insistence on full employment as a guiding objective and their insistence on the necessary complementary interaction between economic growth and social reforms. The particularity of Myrdal's approach was that he regarded overall investment policies as the strategic tool with which governments should manage and orient economic growth. Internationally he advocated that vast credit resources should be provided from richer countries (Sweden and above all the United States) in order to achieve a concerted and cooperative post-war reconstruction. These guiding principles retain their full relevance in the present international economic and social crisis, particularly when confronting the dilemmas of the European Union.

Myrdal's ideas are consequently extremely relevant. But we need to go beyond his ideas in order assert the legitimacy of democratic institutions to harness and regulate finance and business interests. The social irresponsibility of finance can no longer be condoned. A new understanding of the mechanics of credit creation – of democracy, of reasoned public approval as a basis for sustainable credit – will also enable the creation of new financial instruments capable of financing long-term growth – ecologically oriented and cooperative – in the member countries of the European Union and beyond.

Between morality and realism: the ideas of Gunnar Myrdal in the new international political landscape

The ideas above have been developed from a rational point of view. But when is rational thinking and action possible? This is a problem with which Myrdal struggled all his life. In his early years it was almost as if he thought that the mere demonstration of a rational idea would suffice to convince Swedish business interests of the inevitability of economic planning and welfare societies. In his study on US race relations during the war he recognized the strength of racial prejudice but nevertheless held a firm belief in people's individual desire to be honest, logic and consistently rational. Myrdal noticed each individual held different valuations, these valuations often conflicted, and when they did the more timeless and general ones were considered to be morally higher. This was the basis for his appeal to the 'American Creed' of equality of opportunity to combat racial prejudices in public opinion and amongst the liberal elites. This moral dimension was also very prominent when he wanted Western public opinion – and particularly US liberal opinion – to address the challenges of international inequalities and world poverty in the late 1960s. But – as other biographers of Myrdal have noted – he grew considerably more disillusioned in his later years. Even if he was insistently aware of the 'opportunistic bias' of knowledge, and the tendency to hide valuation conflicts and rationalized given beliefs and valuations, he overestimated the capacity of social sciences and of public debates in Western societies to correct distorted beliefs.

His excessive optimism is especially true regarding his appeal to public opinion in the United States. Forty years after *Challenge of World Poverty* was published the United States is a powerful and threatening giant bent on overconsumption and domination. With 4 per cent of the world's population it accounts for half the world's expenditure on armaments with no apparent rival in sight – and still feels insecure. And the inner social structure of the United States has reached inequality levels not seen since before the 1929 crash. Today, any appeal to 'American Creed' or generosity would appear to the majority of the people of the world as misplaced.

And what of Europe in this context? Is there a moral way out of the 'European Dilemma' presented above? With Myrdal's efforts as Executive Secretary of the UN Commission for Europe in mind, it is reasonable to think that he would have argued for a generous and cooperative effort. An effort aimed at furthering the economic integration of the EU as a way out of the present dilemma. The propositions developed above lead very much in the same direction. But what of their realism? Are such cooperative initiatives realistic?

If past experiences are anything to judge by, then probably not. The forces of entrenched interests in the institutions of and around the European Union have been enormously resilient in resisting any call for a change of orientation, especially since the outbreak of public debt crises in the financially more vulnerable countries of the Union. The responses so far have rather reinforced the authoritarian mechanisms of the decision-making procedures by the so-called 'Six-Pack Pact', depriving national parliaments of their independence on economic policies, making a troika of representatives from the European Commission, the European Central Bank and the International Monetary Fund into some kind of super-governors.

To note this authoritarian turn is not to argue that the moral element in politics is unimportant, or that the search for rational solutions on moral challenges is in vain. But nevertheless there appears to be a fundamental flaw in Myrdal's appeal to the moral conscience of liberal opinions on both sides of the Atlantic as he doesn't specify the context needed for this appeal to be followed by action. The question should be reframed: when are the powerful ready to listen to rational arguments?

If we pursue another line of Myrdal's thinking, his insistence on hard-boiled realist analysis, a tentative answer to this question would be: the mighty are ready to listen only when forced to by powerful social forces.

This implies the necessary link between socially concerned scientists and social movements. It is only when carried by social movements of various kinds – trade unions, feminist and ecologist movements, solidarity movements – that 'rational' solutions can make headway into governing institutions.

This conclusion means taking a step away from the 'elitist' bias in Gunnar Myrdal's approach to the belief that Social Sciences must be deeply implicated in a dialogue with disempowered groups in order to be a tool for social change. In Europe this dialogue is already well under way: the convergence of trade unions and the myriad of organizations involved in the social forums are an indispensable social laboratory in developing new projects for another way of creating Europe. And there is another, heterodox research community of economists engaged in the battle: the *Euro Memorandum Group*, *Attac*, *les Economistes Atterrés* and the *European Progressive Economists' Network* to name only a few.

This ongoing dialogue provides a necessary fermentation for new rationalities. Still, if a guess could be ventured, it is not by overall proposition but by unilateral actions that the actual neo-liberal cage of economic restrictions can be destroyed. Only a government carried by a strong public approval will be able to defy the present destructive constitutional rules and open a way for new social and economic dynamics.

There are factors outside Europe that may allow some degree of optimism. Gunnar Myrdal repeatedly reminded his audience that: history is always open. Take the example of South America, 15 years ago it was crippled by the burden of debt and ruled by right-wing and dictatorial regimes imposing neo-liberal doctrines. At present it is a continent searching for its independence, increasing its regional integration while each country is following its own path to combat inequality and strengthen democracy.

There is also the growing multi-polarity of the world to take into account, with new growth centres in Asia, South America and Africa that may provide space to a Europe trying to establish other links than those based on colonial relations or subservience to financial interests.

As John Kenneth Galbraith wrote: Gunnar Myrdal's ideas 'defined the time and the century, including what has gone wrong'. That century and that period is now gone, but the Enlightenment ideas he carried – the values of rationality, equality and democracy – retain all their strength.

Notes

1 'Struggling Lehman Plans to Lay Off 1.500', *New York Times* 29 August 2008.
2 International Monetary Fund: *World Economic Outlook: Sustaining Recovery.* October 2009. www.imf.org/external/pubs/ft/weo/2009/02/.
3 Same report, Table 1.1.
4 Table presented by Nicolas Crafts and Peter Fearon in *Oxford Review of Economic Policy*, Vol. 26, No 3. BBC Stephanie Flanders: 'Is it the 30s – or the 70s?'.BBC News, 23 December 2010.
5 Eurostat unemployment statistics. Data up to July 2013. http://epp.eurostat. ec.europa.eu/statistics_explained/index.php/Unemployment_statistics.
6 Andrew G. Haldane: 'The $100 billion question'. Published 6 April 2010. www.bis.org/review/r100406d.pdf.
7 The summary is made by BBC economist Steven Schifferes based on the IMF report ahead of the G20 meeting in September 2009. 'Crisis cost us $10,000 each', 10 September 2009. http://news.bbc.co.uk/2/hi/business/8248434.stm.
8 The international currency system established after the war, managed by the International Monetary Fund, is usually referred to as the *Bretton Woods System*, because it was established at a conference in Bretton Woods, USA in 1944.
9 BIS, *Triennial Central Bank Survey: Foreign Exchange and Derivatives Activities*. June 2010. www.bis.org/publ/otc_hy1011.htm.
10 For more details, see International Panel on Climate Change at www.ipcc.ch/.
11 The countries promised to reduce their CO_2 levels of 1990 by 20per cent in 2012. www.unfcc.int.
12 Published in *New York Times*, 2 September 2009. The column later was the basis for an on-line petition demanding an overhaul of the discipline, supported by several thousand economists.
13 The report of this *Commission on the Measurement of Economic Performance and Social Progress* is available at www.stiglitz-sen-fitoussi.fr.
14 The increased 'cost of capital' in France 1996–2010 was recently documented in Laurent Cordonnier et al., 'Le coût du capital et son surcoût. Sens de la notion, mesure et evolution, consequences économiques'. Published by Centre Lillois d'Etudes et de Recherches Economiques et Sociologiques (CLERES), available at http://www.ires-fr.org/images/files/EtudesAO/rapportCgtCoutCapitalK.pdf.
15 www.taxjustice.net.
16 Ann Hollingshead: 'The Implied Tax Revenue Loss from Trade Mispricing', February 2010. *Global Financial Integrity* www.gfintegrity.org.
17 Ann Hollingshead: 'Privately Held Non-Resident Deposits in Secrecy Jurisdictions'. March 2010. *Global Financial Integrity* www.gfintegrity.org.
18 *Tax Justice Network* is a European research organization with a long-standing expertise in these matters. www.taxjustice.net.
19 According to official French statistics (INSEE) presented in Örjan Appelqvist, 'The Continuing Crisis of the Euro – a Weak Link in the Global Financial System?' *Ensaios FEE* Vol. 33, No 2 (2012).
20 The historical background and contemporary use of this concept is developed on the site of CADTM, a research institute working for the annulment of the public debts of Third World countries. www.cadtm-org/dette-odieuse.
21 *Global Economic Growth Report*, Toronto, July 2003. Referred to in François Chesnais, *Les dettes illégitimes. Quand les banques font main basse sur les politiques publiques* (Paris: Raisons d'agir, 2011).

22 The audit resulted in an agreement by which recovered government bonds at a nominal value of US$3.2 billion at a cost of US$1 billion. Total estimated gain for Ecuador amounted to US$7 billion. Jacques Cossart et al., *Le piège de la dette* (Paris: LLL, 2011), p. 37.
23 Frédéric Lordon, *La crise de trop* (Paris: Fayard, 2009).
24 The figures are not strictly comparable: the GDP gives a measure of the overall activities of the real economies whereas the total volume of financial trading rather gives an indication of the volume of daily trading, and thereby the level of risks involved.
25 According to senior BIS economist Morten Bech in a research paper published in 2012. 'Currency Trading of $5 Trillion a Day Surpasses Pre-Lehman High, BIS Says'. bloomberg.com/news/2012–03–11.
26 The latest yearly memorandum, 'The deepening crisis in the European Union. The need for a fundamental change'is available at www.euromemo.eu.
27 Guy Verhofstadt, et al., 'A Plan to Save the Euro, and Curb the Speculators', *Financial Times*, 4 July; Stuart Holland, 'Solid Reasons why Eurobonds can be made to Work', *Financial Times*, 16 August 2011.

Bibliography

Works by Gunnar and Alva Myrdal

Myrdal, G., *Prisbildningsproblemet och föränderligheten* (Stockholm: Almqvist & Wicksell, 1927).

Vetenskap och politik i nationalekonomien (Stockholm: Norstedts, 1930).

Sveriges väg genom penningkrisen (Stockholm: Natur och Kultur, 1931).

'Om penningteoretisk jämvikt: en studie over den "normala räntan" I Wicksells penninglära', *Ekonomisk Tidskrift* in 1931.

Konjunktur och offentlig hushållning. En utredning (Stockholm: Kooperativa föbundets bokförlag, 1933).

'Den förändrade världsbilden inom nationalekonomien' in *Krisen och samhällsvetenskaperna. Två installationsföreläsningar* (Stockholm: Kooperativa Förbundet,1935).

Jordbrukspolitiken under omläggning (1938).

Monetary Equilibrium (London: W. Hodge & Co Ltd,1939).

'Fiscal Policy in the Business Cycle', *American Economic Review*, 1939.

Varning för Fredsoptimism [*Warning against Post-War Optimism*] (Stockholm: Bonniers, 1944).

'Höga skatter och låga räntor', *Studier i Ekonomi och Historia.Tillägnade Eli f. Heckscher* (Stockholm: Bonniers, 1944).

An American Dilemma: The Negro Problem and Modern Democracy. Vols. 1 and 2 (New York: Harper & Brothers, 1944).

'Staten och industrin' [*The State and the Industry*]. Speech made on 8 January 1946 to Stockholm's Köpmannaklubb (Association of Stockholm Merchants), published in *Industria*, Vol. 42, 1946.

The Political Element in the Development of Economic Theory (London: Routledge and Kegan Paul, 1953).

An International Economy: Problems and Prospects (New York: Harper, 1956).

Economic Theory and Under-developed Regions (London: Duckworth, 1957).

Rich Lands and Poor (New York: Harper & Row, 1957).

'De internationella organisationerna', *Svenska Dagbladet*, 15 October 1957.

'Det internationella samarbetets brister', *Svenska Dagbladet* 15 October 1957.

Asian Drama: An Inquiry onto the Poverty of Nations (New York: Twentieth Century Fund, 1968).

Objectivity in Social Research: The Wimmer Lectures (New York: Pantheon Books, 1969).

The Challenge of World Poverty: A World Anti-Poverty Program in Outline (New York: Pantheon Books, 1970).

'Economics of an Improved Environment'. Lecture delivered in connection with the United Nations Conference on the Human Environment, 8 June 1972, Stockholm, in M. F. Strong (ed.), *Who Speaks for Earth?* (New York, 1973).

'Increasing Interdependence between STATes but Failure of International Cooperation', *Felix Neubergh Lecture*, Göteborg 1977. Vol. XII, No. 4, December 1978.

'Behovet av reformer i under-utvecklande länder', *Världspolitikens dagsfrågor*, 1978, p. 10.

'The Need for Reforms in Underdeveloped Countries', lecture given in August 1978.

'Institutional Economics' in *Journal of Economic Issues*, Vol. XII, No. 4, 1978.

—— Alva Myrdal, *Stickprov från Storbritannien* (Stockholm, Bonniers, 1942).

Other contributions

Adler-Karlsson, G., *Western Economic Warfare 1947–1967: A Case Study in Foreign Economic Policy* (Stockholm: Almqvist & Wiksell, 1968).

Angresano, J., *The Political Economy of Gunnar Myrdal: An Institutional Basis for the Transformation Problem* (Cheltenham: Edward Elgar, 1997).

Appelqvist, Ö., *Bruten Brygga. Gunnar Myrdal och Sveriges ekonomiska efterkrigspolitik 1943–1947* (Stockholm: Santérus, 2000).

Appelqvist, Ö., 'A Hidden Duel: Gunnar Myrdal and Dag Hammarskjöld in Economics and International Politics 1935–1955', *Stockholm Papers in Economic History (SWoPEc)*, No 2. (2008).

Appelqvist, Ö., 'Prebisch and Myrdal: Development Economics in the core and on the Periphery', *Journal of Global History*, Vol. 6, 2011.

Appelqvist, Ö., 'The Continuing Crisis of the Euro – a Weak Link in the Global Financial System?' *Ensaios FEE*, Vol. 33, No. 2 (2012).

Appelqvist, Ö., '*Keynes et le socialisme démocratique en Suède* in D. Cohen and A. Bergougnioux (eds), *Le socialisme à l'épreuve du capitalisme* (Paris: Fayard, 2012).

Appelqvist, Ö. and S. Andersson (eds), *The Essential Gunnar Myrdal* (New York: New Press, 2005).

Arrighi, G., *Adam Smith in Beijing: Lineages of the Twentyfirst Century* (London: Verso, 2007).

Barber, W.J., *Gunnar Myrdal: An Intellectual Biography* (London: Palgrave, 2008).

Borgström, G., *Gränser för vår tillvaro [Limits to our Existence]* (Stockholm: LT, 1967).

Borgström, G., *The Hungry Planet: The Modern World at the Edge of Famine* (New York: Macmillan, 1965).

Cassel, G., *Theory of Social Economy* (London: Fisher Unwin, 1923).

Chesnais, F., *Les dettes illégitimes. Quand les banques font main basse sur les politiques publiques* (Paris: Raisons d'agir, 2011).

Cossart, J. *et al.*, *Le piège de la dette* (Paris: LLL, 2011), p. 37.

Dostaler, G., 'Les grands auteurs de la pensée économique', *Alternatives économiques, Hors-série Poche*, No. 57, Novembre 2012, pp. 138–141.

Dostaler, G., D. Ethier and L. Lepage (eds), *Gunnar Myrdal and his Works* (Montreal: Harvest House Publishers, 1992).

Haldane, A., 'The $100 Billion Question', www.bis.org/review/r100406d.pdf

Hirdman, Y., *Alva Myrdal: The Passionate Mind* (Bloomington, IN: Indiana University Press, 2008).

Hollingshead, A., 'The Implied Tax Revenue Loss from Trade Mispricing'. February 2010. *Global Financial Integrity*, www.gfintegrity.org.

Hollingshead, A., 'Privately Held Non-resident Deposits in Secrecy Jurisdictions'. March 2010. *Global Financial Integrity*, www.gfintegrity.org.

Hirst, P. and G. Thompson, *Globalization in Question* (Cambridge: Polity Press, 1999).

Jackson, W.A., *Gunnar Myrdal and America's Conscience: Social Engineering and Racial Liberalism 1938–1987* (Chapel Hill: University of North Carolina Press, 1990).

Karlsson, B., *Handelspolitik eller politisk handling. Sveriges handel med öststaterna 1946–1952* (Göteborg: Ekonomisk-historiska institutionen, 1992).

Kostelecký, V., *UN Economic Commission for Europe: The Beginning of a History* (Göteborg: Landsorganisationen, 1989).

Lordon, F., *La crise de trop* (Paris: Fayard, 2009).

Lorwin, L.L., *Det andra världskriget och dess ekonomiska följder* (Stockholm: Bonniers, 1942).

Minsky, H., *Stabilizing an Unstable Economy* (New Haven, CT: Yale University Press, 1986).

Milward, S., *The Reconstruction of Western Europe 1945–51* (Cambridge: Cambridge University Press, 1987).

Misgeld, K., *Die 'Internationale gruppe Demokratischer Sozialisten' in Stockholm 1942–1945. Zur sozialistischen Friedensdiskussion während des Zweitens Weltkrieges* (Uppsala: 1976).

Ohlin, B., *Interregional and International Trade* (Cambridge, MA: Harvard University Press, 1932).

Palmstierna, H., *Svält, plundering, förgiftning* (Famine, Plunder, Poisoning) (Stockholm: Rabén & Sjögren,1967).

Sevòn, C., *Vägen till EuropaSvensk neutralitet och europeisk återuppbyggnad 1945* (Helsinki: Suomen historiallinen seura, 1995).

Stiglitz, J., *Globalization and its Discontents* (London: Allen Lane/Penguin Books, 2002).

Stiglitz, J., A. Sen and J.-P. Fitoussi, 'Commission on the Measurement of Economic Performance and Social Progress', www.stiglitz-sen-fitoussi.fr.

Skidelsky, R., *Keynes: The Return of the Master* (London: Allen Lane, 2009).

Svennilson, I., *Growth and Stagnation in the European Economy* (Geneva: UNECE, 1954).

Toye, J. and R. Toye, *The United Nations and the Global Political Economy: Trade, Finance and Development* (Bloomington, IN: Indiana University Press, 2004).

Taleb, N.N., *The Black Swan: The Impact of the Highly Improbable* (London: Allen Lane 2007).

United Nations Intellectual History Project (UNIHP), *Reflections on United Nations Development Ideas: Proceedings of Conference on 24 January 2005 in Geneva – From Development to Governance* (New York: UNIHP).

Verhofstadt, G. *et al.*, 'A Plan to Save the Euro and Curb Speculators', *Financial Times*, 4 July 2011.

Further sources

Attac, www.attac.org

Bank for International Settlements, Triennial Surveys, www.bis.org

Committee for the Abolishment of the Third World Debt, www.cadtm.org

EuroMemorandum Group, www.euromemo.eu

Eurostat, http://epp.eurostat.ec.europa.eu

Global Financial Integrity, www.gintegrity.org

International Monetary Fund, World Economic Outlook, www.imf.org

Tax Justice Network, www.taxjustice.net

Index

public sector, role in economy 26–35,
36
public works 28–9

quantitative easing 111, 128
quantitative theory on monetary policy
6

race relations, US 12–13, 35, 131
rationalism 12, 96, 99, 118, 131, 133
rationalization 99; of industry 43
raw materials *see* primary products
rearmament, US 60
regulation school 110, 117
reproduction 37, 120
reproduction costs of real capital 23
resources: depletion 83, 85, 86, 87, 88,
95, 113; distribution of 87–8, 91, 95;
international trade in 87, see also
primary products
Rich Lands and Poor 78, 99
Riksbanken 60
risk analysis 19, 22
Rivarola, Andrés 81
Robbins, Lionel 55
Roosevelt, Franklin D. 54
running expenditures 31, 130
Russia, currency crisis (1998) 106

Sack, Alexander 125
Safe Haven-negotiations 62
savings 23, 24, 29
scarcity of primary products 55
science: natural 7, 114; *see also* social
sciences
Sen, Amartya 117
shareholder value 121
Six-Pack Pact 132
Skidelsky, Robert 22
small nations versus great powers 59
Smith, Adam 6
Social Democrats, Sweden 27, 30, 36,
42, 44, 50–1
social market economy 67
social movements 132
social policy/reform 24, 25, 28–9, 36,
37, 39, 40, 42, 45, 130
social safety nets 120, 121
social sciences 7–8, 132; linguistic turn
in 13; objectivity in 11–12;

scientifically naïve method in 9, 10,
11, 21; and society 10–11; value-
critical method in 9, 10, 11, 15
socialism 37, 42
socialization 43
soft state 76, 78
Soros, George 107
soundness in public finance 31–2, 34,
39
South America 2, 106, 111, 133
South Asia 111; population growth 75,
77; social development 3, 12–13,
73–7
South Korea 111
Soviet bloc 93
Soviet Union 52, 55, 58, 60, 61, 62
Spain 112; unemployment 106
speculation 109, 112, 128
Sri Lanka 74
stagflation 95, 104n116
state: intervention 43, 67; minimal
(`night-watch') 27; role in
development 70, 76; soft 76, 78
static equilibrium hypothesis 16
stickiness 17, 19; wages 6, 24
Stiglitz, Joseph 21, 117
stock markets 26, 105, 106, 109
Stockholm School of Economists 9
Structural Adjustment Programs 81,
124
structural unemployment 6, 118
sub-prime mortage market 22, 108
supply, and demand 6, 85
Swedish Employers Association (SAF)
42
Swedish–Soviet Credit and Trade
Agreement 44, 62, 100–1n35

Taleb, Nassim 22
tax 29, 41, 45, 121, 122; evasion
122–3; US 54
Tax Justice Network 123
technological advance: in agriculture
78, 81, 83; and ecological crisis 115;
in industry 83
Third World 21, 47n32
time dimension: and ecological
problems 85, 91; in neo-classical
economics 19–23, 85; and price
formation process 17

For Product Safety Concerns and Information please contact our
EU representative GPSR@taylorandfrancis.com Taylor & Francis
Verlag GmbH, Kaufingerstraße 24, 80331 München, Germany